BLUE MESA REVIEW

Rudolfo A. Anaya, Editor
David Johnson, Guest Editor

The Creative Writing Center
at the University of New Mexico

Spring 1990

BLUE MESA REVIEW

Editor: Rudolfo A. Anaya

Guest Editor: David Johnson

Editorial Board: Gene Frumkin
                  Patricia Clark Smith
                  Luci Tapahonso

Managing Editor: Uma Kukathas

Editorial Assistants: Alan Blackstock, Susan Engman, Ed Lorusso, Kate Marsters, Paul Olson, Diane Wegmann

Published by the Creative Writing Center, Department of English, University of New Mexico

BLUE MESA REVIEW is published annually

Funding for BLUE MESA REVIEW was provided by the University of New Mexico's College of Arts and Sciences, the Urban Enhancement Cultural Achievement Project of the City of Albuquerque, the Graduate Student Association.

Subscriptions are $10 per year. Individuals and institutions please order from
        BLUE MESA REVIEW Subscriptions
        English Department
        University of New Mexico
        Albuquerque, NM 87131

Bookstores please order from
        The University of New Mexico Press
        Journalism Building
        University of New Mexico
        Albuquerque, NM 87131
        (505) 277-7564

Manuscripts should be sent to BLUE MESA REVIEW, Department of English, University of New Mexico, Albuquerque, NM 87131. Only those manuscripts accompanied by a self-addressed, stamped envelope will be returned.

Cover shows a watercolor painting by Todd B. Tibbals, "Church Plaza." For information about Mr. Tibbals' work, please write to him at 7316 Guadalupe Trail NW, Los Ranchos de Albuquerque, New Mexico.

Copyright 1990 by the Creative Writing Center of the University of New Mexico
ISSN 1042-2951

Contents

Introduction / vii
The Beige Cow / *Mahlon Murphy* / 1
Three poems / *Ray Gonzalez* / 15
Two poems / *Joel Friederich* / 20
Two poems / *Peter Wild* / 22
His City / *Christopher Woods* / 24
Zeros in Mine / *Anthony Wallace* / 27
Stomping with Pettit on the Battenkill / *Garrett Kaoru Hongo* / 28
The Disciple / *Melissa Miller* / 30
Lightning Stork / *Susan Barnett* / 32
Two poems / *Robert Burlingame* / 34
Las Cruces and Five Lost Years / *Albino Carillo* / 36
Black and White / *Carlos Nicolas Flores* / 38
ease / *Sylvia Giron* / 63
Science / *Henry Rael, Jr.* / 64
Evolution by Night / *Eryc Bourland* / 66
Why it is better to read some afternoons / *Judi Lynne Judy* / 68
Dream Fragment Thirty / *Roy Ricci* / 69
Two poems / *L. V. Quintana* / 70
Santorini / *James Ruppert* / 72
Two poems / *Bayita Garoffolo* / 74
Colors in the Valley / *James Mackie* / 76
Points of Departure / *Jeffrey N. Johns* / 77
Two poems / *Alicia Gaspar de Alba* / 81
Picking up the License / *J. Dianne Duff* / 84
Oscar Comes Through New Mexico from El Salvador /
    Maisha Baton / 86

dare to un-do masks / *Mark Funk* / 88

The Visitor / *Layle Silbert* / 89

Two poems / *Miriam McCluney* / 97

Two poems / *Joy Harjo* / 100

Belated Visit / *David Ray* / 104

The Fire-bird / *Harvena Richter* / 106

Two poems / *Levi Romero* / 108

Sombras de la Jicarita / *Gabriel Melendez* / 111

Berkana / *Wilma Rodriguez* / 117

Two poems / *Deborah Muldavin* / 118

White Buffalo Woman / *Jeane Jacobs* / 121

Three Songs of the Medicine Bundle / *James Thomas Stevens* / 128

Medea in Taos / *James Hoggard* / 130

Two poems / *Sandra Blystone* / 132

Body Identified / *Laura Tohe* / 135

The Wall / *John Martinez Weston* / 136

Apartment #4 / *Penelope Gillen* / 140

To the Point / *Mercedes Lawry* / 141

The Photographer / *Carmela Delia Lanza* / 142

The Prediction / *Alicia Gaspar de Alba* / 144

Manon Welcomes the Return of the Hot Season / *Martha Elizabeth* / 151

Stars / *Brian Swann* / 152

The Other Grandma / *Tricia Baatz* / 153

Compression: An Essay in Stanzas / *David E. Hailey, Jr.* / 166

Listening to Bill Drinkard / *Thomas Alan Holmes* / 171

Ma / *Michael Arvey* / 172

Two poems / *Jeane E. Clark* / 174

Flying / *Shuli Lamden* / 178

Two poems / *J. Mills* / 181

Two poems / *Miriam Sagan* / 184

How to Accommodate Men / *Marilyn Krysl* / 186

BOOK REVIEWS

Gene Frumkin
Surface Tension, by Elaine Equi / 197
Unexpected Grace; Diving Through Light, by Glenna Luschei / 199
Here, by Glenna Luschei / 201
A New Path to the Waterfall, by Raymond Carver / 203

Patricia Clark Smith
Good Books, Briefly / 206

Notes on Contributors / 208

Editors' Note

We are pleased to publish the winners of the 1990 Urban Enhancement Cultural Achievement Awards for Fiction and Poetry in this issue of BLUE MESA REVIEW. The award winner in poetry is Levi Romero, for "Tres Copas de Chanate: Black and Sweet." Mahlon Murphy wins the fiction prize for his story "The Beige Cow." Other winners:

Poetry	2nd place	Miriam McCluney	"Crossings"
Poetry	Honorable mention	Laura Tohe	"Body Identified"
Fiction	2nd place	Carlos Nicolas Flores	"Black and White"
Fiction	Honorable mention	Gabriel Melendez	"Sombras de la Jicarita"

Our thanks to the City of Albuquerque's Cultural Achievement Project for sponsoring this contest.

Issue number three of BLUE MESA REVIEW is scheduled for publication in the Spring of 1991. The issue's theme will be "La Frontera." The theme will be a special section; we continue to welcome all submissions. Deadline for submissions is August 31, 1990. Manuscripts should be sent to BLUE MESA REVIEW, Department of English, University of New Mexico, Albuquerque, NM 87131.

BLUE MESA REVIEW is funded by the College of Arts and Sciences and the Graduate Student Association at the University of New Mexico.

Introduction

A Lakota Indian legend tells of an old woman who sits in the moonlight weaving the tapestry of the world with porcupine quills. Nearby a kettle of herbs is boiling over a fire. A dog watches her. Occasionally she leaves her work and stirs the herbs. Then the dog gets up, goes over to her weaving and unravels it. She returns to the tapestry and begins again. This has been going on for thousands of years. If she ever completes her work, the world will end.

In one form or another this image of the woman weaving together reality is repeated throughout the world. Sometimes it is the spider woman (Grandmother Spider or Cosmic Spider) who creates the web of life out of her own body, and connects all the various parts of nature with her delicate threads. All the mother goddesses of the ancient world were spinners and weavers exerting their influence on fate or destiny. The thread of the Great Weaver is the umbilical cord which attaches each individual to the creator as well as to the world tapestry into which each destiny is woven. The tapestry or spider's web is a microcosm of the unity of the world.

Weaving has become one of the basic metaphors for individual creativity and for the ongoing creation of the cosmos. Symbolically, the warp represents the vertical plane: our transcendent concerns, the spiritual dimension, and timeless principles. The weft or woof represents the horizontal plane: the day to day existence of things in time and space, the material dimension. Each crossing of the warp and woof symbolizes a coming together of two dimensions and the reconciliation of opposites: the joining of time and eternity, spirit and matter, day and night.

A blanket made by a traditional weaver illustrates another kind of synthesis. In addition to physical warmth, the weave and symbolic design of a blanket embody the vision of its maker and the powers of nature, thus providing strength and protection to the person using it. A Navajo blanket, for example, is a blend of art, craft, and religion, reflecting an intermingling of the material and the spiritual, the sacred and the secular.

The weaving metaphor applies to all the arts, but in *Blue Mesa Review* it is particularly appropriate to writing. The writer, like the spider at the center of his own creativity, spins a web of relationships, attaching one image to another: a butterfly to a rock, an ancestor to a neighborhood, a fleeting memory to a wall—from inside to outside, and back again. This delicate, tenuous web needs constant attention and regular repair in order to support us as human beings.

The planet itself is threatened unless we support and celebrate the value of this creative activity and embrace the truth of the organic paradigm which underlies it. An excerpt from a speech by Chief Seattle in 1852 is an eloquent statement of this view of reality:

> This we know. The earth does not belong to man, man belongs to the earth. This we know. All things are connected like the blood which unites one family. All things are connected. Whatever befalls the earth befalls the sons of earth. Man did not weave the web of life, he is merely a strand in it. Whatever he does to the web, he does to himself.

The final goal of all inspired writing is to create a community of the living, an inclusive and caring community, which, being by being, species by species, expands into a global perspective. It shares these functions with all the other arts, with mythology, religion, music and dream.

David Johnson, Guest Editor

The Beige Cow

MAHLON MURPHY

The sea took most of it. The jungle came and took the rest.

It was a ruin, a decomposition of what had been a grand estate. But Gerald didn't care about that. He didn't care about anything.

The villagers finally lost their patience with Gerald. Still, they took pity on him, they were not cruel. After all, hadn't the man lost his wife and his daughter? Hadn't he told them the story a hundred times?

After days and nights of drinking and making a nuisance of himself, the villagers felt they had to do something with Gerald.

Unconscious and stinking like a rotten thing, he was placed on a truck and hauled off to the ruin. They did it quietly, nonchalantly, as if it were the customary way of dealing with a creature like him.

When Gerald opened his eyelids he didn't know he was awake. He thought he was inside a dream, that he would come out of it somehow, sometime, his previous life intact—.

"Aguardiente!" he shouted.

No reply. Only the distant sound of waves breaking on a shore.

"Aguardiente!"

Gerald barked out his orders in the bare room, a bone white enclosure with no roof. Recumbent in white sand, he cried for more whiskey.

The villagers had placed a tattered blanket over him. Oyster shells and shards of crusty roof tiles lay scattered about.

The jungle entered through window openings, a single doorway, and over the top of the walls. Thorny brush with red flowers and green vines as tough as hemp grew out of sand and rubble.

A beige cow stood in the doorway.

The cow gazed at Gerald. Cautiously, it took a few steps forward, crossed the threshold. It browsed on flowers and broad green leaves. It was of the brahma type: its back was hunched and its head was thin, angular, and bony. Its ears were large, set low on the head, and flickered now and then, scooping the air like small propellers.

Gerald thought the beige cow was a bartender.

"Aguardiente!"

He was proud of his ability to enunciate so strange a word, one of a dozen Spanish words he knew. He began to realize that he was horizontal to the world. But he didn't care. It was all part of a dream, anyway, just another movie in the mind.

"Tequila, then, you lazy bastard!"

He shouted for a long time at the cow. Then he heard a reply.

"Shut up!" A woman's voice. From far away, it seemed to him, but nonetheless distinct, angry, gruff, yes, an intrusion from afar, a rudeness. How dare a woman's voice—his wife's?—blast into his private silent documentary for men only—.

"Hey mama!" Gerald yelled. "What's your problem?"

No answer. Only the background surf.

The beige cow bit into a vine and spun its propellers. It turned its bony rump on Gerald.

Lying on the sand with cracked tiles, sinewy vines, and pools of his own vomit about him, Gerald laughed out loud.

"You're not the goddamned cantinero," he said. "You're a cow. Holy cow! How now, holy cow!"

Gerald nearly choked on his own laughter.

A contingent of flies from the buzzing colony of flies hovering over him migrated to the cow. In response the brahma swished its tail back and forth, back and forth, a rhythm steady as the metronome on his wife's piano.

Gerald tried to make his eyes behave, to focus on the cow's tail.

"Toro, toro!" he said.

He'd be brave, bravo. Nothing to lose anyway. Just a dream. A movie. He'd be a matador with this bull that was a cow.

He had to get himself vertical, though. No easy task in his condition. His vision was cloudy. He had no equilibrium, only a sense of vertigo.

Gerald fixed his sights on the tail as it flip-flopped in front of him. Summoning all his strength and power of concentration, he made a bold lurch forward with both arms, groping like a blindfolded child, his daughter at her birthday piñata.

Gerald caught the tail, just barely, by the black tuft of its tip.

Wide-eyed, horrified, the beige cow bucked up its butt. It kicked, snorted, jerked and twisted its loose flesh in every direction. It trampled flowers and bushes and stumbled through a network of vines and fractured tiles.

Gerald hung on. He would not let go.

"Toro! Toro!"

His body, already a mass of contusions, sustained new insults. Still he hung on, he felt no pain, he didn't care.

A line from his wife's favorite song came to the wounded toreador: *Don't it make my brown eyes blue. Don't it make my brown eyes blue.* What did it mean?

The beige cow lumbered about the room. It moaned. It shit all over Gerald. Still he hung on. A watery lymph covered him.

Twice the beige cow circled the enclosure. Then it found its way out the door and bolted into the jungle.

When Gerald let go he was lying immobile in green muck that buried him, an atmosphere of polished cable-like vines and leaves the size of tabloids. A spiral of gnats buzzed his mouth. Everything was slick, wet, viscous with pulse.

He lay still, awake, heavy with fear and nausea, the jungle doing to him what it wanted.

He lifted his head from the green mud. With his arms he flailed at the chaos in front of his face.

In a small clearing, just above him, he saw the fierce grey eyes of a dark, sweaty woman bearing down on him.

"You incredible asshole," she said.

It was the same voice as before, the one that had broken the dream for men only.

The jungle blinked a darkness over Gerald. He was aware only of the sensation of drowning in murky, briny water. Large fish swam about him, unperturbed. In their open jaws were the faces of women.

The voice of a girl came to Gerald when he woke up. The singing came from another room, separated from his by a curtained doorway. He was lying on a soft, clean bed. There was darkness except for the barest light filtering through the curtain. The girl's voice reminded him of his own daughter, nine years old and far away, he didn't know where.

He listened to her song. He heard metal sounds also, and wood sounds. And the woman's voice.

"Amanda, come over here, sweetheart. I want you to read to me while I make dinner. Okay?"

"Okay."

Gerald sat up. His body hurt. His limbs ached. His head felt like an unripe coconut. Heavy juice sloshed back and forth between his ears. His eyes felt like swollen marbles. But he could see straight. His vision was no longer cloudy.

That is lovely, he thought as he listened to the girl. Here I am, God knows where, and a little girl is reading poetry to her mother.

When he stood up a fine alpaca blanket slipped away from him, falling to the floor. He saw that he was stark naked. He recalled the woman's voice in the watery jungle. The severity of her wet face, the grey punitive eyes. The beige cow was there too, a picture, a blurry image in the fog of his memory. And his wife's face in the mouth of a fish. Drowning without pain. . . .

Gerald ran a hand over his chest and belly.

Something was different. He was clean, trim, purged. He felt a sudden, overwhelming shame.

He sat on the edge of the bed, quiet, stealing glances at the light through the patterned curtain, listening to the pots and pans and the poetry.

Into the darkness about him came the smell of wood burning and the aroma of spices. He thought of his wife. Twelve years together, a good marriage. What happened? Everything going for him. Beautiful wife. Beautiful daughter. Beautiful home. His promotion to regional chief. Everything. What happened?

For an hour Gerald sat, perfectly still, listening to the words of the girl, the poetry in English and Spanish. The kitchen sounds. The laughter as they ate and talked. It was good to sit still, to not disturb the liquid between his ears.

When the woman came and pulled back the curtain, the light nearly blinded him.

"Anything alive in here?" she asked.

"Yes," said Gerald. "More or less."

"Well, there's food out here if you're hungry."

"Thank you. Uh, where's my clothes?" Gerald stood up with the blanket wrapped around him.

"Your clothes are gone. You lost them to the sea."

The wave of shame hit him again.

The light accented the woman's thin silhouette with the thick cascade of kinky hair. The luminescent glow of her eyes made Gerald pause before saying anything.

"Tomorrow," said the woman. "I'll bring you some clothes from the village." She let the curtain drop and walked away. The light seemed to go with her.

"And then," he heard her add, "then you can leave."

When he stepped out of the dark room, covered in the blanket, Gerald felt revived by the warmth of the kitchen, the delicious smells. On a table were set plates of rice and shrimp, a bowl of black beans, and a pot of tea. He was alone in the room. The sound of a piano came from another part of the house.

He sat at the table and devoured everything in front of him.

The woman came into the kitchen. She gestured for Gerald to follow her. Wearing the blanket like a serape, he walked down a wide hallway and followed her into a huge room. The only light came from a bare incandescent bulb dangling on a wire tied to the lower rim of a large wrought iron chandelier. The room's furniture was clustered in a circle beneath the light. Outside the circle, in semi-darkness, was a big, angular, black object.

Gerald tugged his blanket tighter about him. He was embarrassed at his nakedness, at the whiteness and hairiness of his exposed shins. But the magenta floor tiles felt cool and soothing to his feet.

In the dim light the woman possessed an unnatural brightness, a vibrance. But she was not, he thought, beautiful, and it seemed to him in some absurd way that this was an injustice. After all he'd been through—the pain, humiliation, penance—his rescuer (was she not?) ought to be beautiful. As he watched her move about he could not shake the thought.

Her body was thin, dark, lithe like the vines that waited outside. She wore a loose yellow cotton dress. Her hair was long and dark and frizzy, with streaks of grey. Gerald wondered if she was Jewish. Her complexion was brown, but her eyes were like the uncanny grey-blue eyes of malamutes.

"What's your name?" Gerald asked.

"My name is Mercedes. My daughter is Amanda."

"Where is she?"

"Sleeping. It's late, you know."

"Sure. Well, actually I don't have a very good sense of time right now. Where am I, Mercedes?"

"You are in my house. You've been here for two days and one night. Tonight will be the second night."

I don't believe that, Gerald thought.

"Two days!" he said. "That's impossible. Listen, my name is—."

"No. You listen," Mercedes said. "I believe that if a burden of proof exists here, it's with you. But what can you talk about if you don't even know what's going on?"

"Wait! Wait a minute—."

"I really don't care what your name is. That doesn't matter. They brought you here from the village because you're sick."

"I'm fine!"

"They brought you here because you're a gringo, and so am I. They didn't know what to do with you, so they brought you to me."

They? he wondered. They? His drinking buddies. The long drive south, insane with hurt, reckless, passing trucks and buses on treacherous mountain roads, heading for Vallarta where she may be, must be, has to be. The one-horse town on the coast, the cantina for men only, the oblivion of nights, the drinking buddies. What were their names? He could not remember any of their names.

Mercedes turned her back on him. She stepped out of the lit circle, towards the black mass that Gerald thought was some horrid sculpture or something. It was large, roughly rectangular, and appeared to be covered with bark, moss, and tiny stones. The texture was rough, volcanic-looking.

Mercedes put a hand on the object. She played a few bars of a song.

Gerald felt outrage. A trick. It can't be a damn piano! What's happening here?

From somewhere above them came a girl's voice, Amanda, singing along with the piano.

"Amanda!" said Mercedes. "You get to sleep. Right now."

Gerald heard the delightful sound (he knew it from his own daughter) of a girl giggling beneath the bed covers.

Mercedes stood by the piano, smiling to herself. She faced Gerald again, nodded in the direction of a small couch, a wicker settee in poor repair.

Everywhere he looked Gerald saw the crumbling artifacts of elegance. The place had been, at one time, a palatial mansion. What had happened to it?

Clutching his serape Gerald lowered himself onto the loveseat, trying his best to keep his body covered.

Mercedes sat opposite him on a rickety wooden rocker. She studied him as if he were an object.

For an instant Gerald saw the head of a cow at the far end of the piano. The cow peeked around the corner at him, flicked its whirligig ears, and retreated.

Jesus! He sat upright. This place is insane. This woman—.

He directed his gaze to the ceiling and saw . . . the sky. The room had no ceiling. Moonglow. Stars. Sea sounds. Vines draped over the ragged tops of the walls, coming out of the blackness beyond, out of their own shadows. A nausea rose in his chest.

But the light, he thought. The chandelier?

He shielded his eyes from the dangling light bulb. He saw an immense, dense entanglement of vines growing outward, in radial spokes, from the chandelier.

"What the hell *is* this place?" he asked Mercedes.

"This place," she replied, "is our home."

Impossible, he thought. Goddamned bitch.

The thought was there, quick in his mind, floating on the water that would not recede from his head. He saw the thought: a buoyant lump of garbage on green, dead water.

"I mean," he pursued, "well—I mean, uh, what *was* it? What was it before?"

He could barely organize his thoughts. Mercedes stared at him a while longer before she spoke. He felt dissembled.

"A long time ago," she said, "this place was an estate. It belonged to some very rich, very bad people. It was abandoned after a big hurricane came through. Then the jungle pretty much reclaimed it."

"You, uh, you actually *live* here?"

"Yes. I live here. Amanda lives here. Precisely."

"But how? How could you? I mean, to raise a little girl in a place like this?"

Gerald tried to regain some composure, some control of his mind. His entire body ached, his head most intensely.

Mercedes did not answer him. She turned her head to one side, her profile revealing a slight mound to the bridge of her nose, a feature that seemed to Gerald to root her to this place in the jungle. Under the light her hair was a dazzle of rays.

Fucking witch, he thought.

Another piece of detritus floated on the dead water of his mind.

Bitch thoughts.

Witch thoughts.

Gerald was hit with an intense pain in his head. He felt in his inner core that he was shallow and unformed, amorphous in character. The pain was a tidal wave between the ears. Then an earthquake down his spinal column. Was he having convulsions? Then a profound heaviness came over his chest. A heart attack?

Mercedes' eyes were on him.

"You have desecrated this place and this time," she said.

"What!" he exclaimed. "Des—?"

Gerald did his best not to let on that he was debilitated, but the oppression in his chest made it difficult for him to breathe, impossible to talk.

"Let me show you something," Mercedes said.

With great effort Gerald stood up and followed her to the front of the piano. Mercedes laid a hand on the hoary old upright. She caressed it, said something to it in Spanish. Gerald thought he would double over in agony.

"Some thirty years ago," she continued, "there was the big hurricane that I mentioned. The sea came in and took a lot of the fancy things in this house. Took some of the people, too. You could say she 'cleaned house,' so to speak. Well, one day about a year ago, she gave back this piano. Just tossed it right up on the beach. Misha found it."

"Misha?" Gerald asked, breathless.

"Our cow. She loves the ocean. It was right after a big storm. She was missing and we went out to look for her. Amanda found her wading in the *playa*, licking and nosing this old piano. Look at it. It's had a nice long sojourn in the sea, don't you think? A brilliant man from the village cleaned the wires and hammers and restored the keyboard."

Gerald touched the side of the piano. Except for the polished ivory keys, the entire surface consisted of layers of barnacles. In spite of himself he couldn't resist. He plunked a finger down on one of the keys.

From above, as if from the night sky itself, came a burst of laughter.

"Amanda!" Mercedes smiled.

Gerald did not want to deal with any of it: a piano of barnacles, a stupid cow with funny ears, a girl's voice laughing in the sky. It was all he could do to keep himself together, mind and body. The blanket kept slipping down his arms. Whatever dignity, whatever authority he still possessed was fast slipping away. He didn't know how to act. His whole way of life had taught him to strike first, ask questions later. If about to be cornered, go on the offensive, get the upper hand.

"Listen, lady," he said, making himself bold, willing it in spite of the pain. "Listen, my name is Gerald Nordhouse. I am the boss of half a dozen laser-tech plants in the Southwest. I didn't get there playing a bunch of games, you know. Every day I make decisions that would turn someone like you to cream. I mean, I have all sorts of responsibilities that most people never even dream of. I mean . . . I make a quarter mil a year. House in Scottsdale. Condo in Puerto Vallarta. Hell, I've got a beautiful wife. A lovely daughter. I . . . I had . . . I was on my way . . . she—."

Mercedes took his hand, steadied him as he was about to fall, guided him back onto the loveseat.

"Name, rank, serial number," she said. "That stuff doesn't matter here."

Gerald felt lightheaded and drained of energy. He sat and tried to follow Mercedes' movements and speech. She seemed to scurry back and forth, in and out of the light, carrying equipment of some sort. Her voice had a sing-song lilt to it, like a chant.

"Once-upon-a-time," she said, "this place was a home-away-from-home for wayward dictators and their cronies. They came from all over Latin America. And their rich friends from the north. They kept mistresses here, drank a lot, played and partied. And they planned their coups here, too. Business as well as pleasure. It was their secret getaway. Very hidden, very exclusive, very discreet. The club of clubs for the generalíssimos."

Gerald found himself incapable of following both the words and the movements of the woman. He focused his attention on her actions until it dawned on him what she was doing: setting up a make-shift screen with sheets and clothespins, attaching a reel of film to a projector.

"Then came the big storm," she continued. "With very little warning the wind and the water came in and razed the place. The generals and their friends beat it through the jungle in their jeeps. They made it to the landing strip just in time, flew off in their airplane. All the women and servants were left behind in the house. The sea came in and took them. She took the windows and doors and furniture, parts of walls, roofs. She took the piano, too. But as you see, she gave it back."

Mercedes threaded the film into the projector. She took the cord and plugged it into a socket above the lightbulb. She gave the light a few quick twists until it went out.

"Okay. We're ready to roll. Just sit back, enjoy the show. It's a gift."

FILM IN BLACK AND WHITE

The film is ancient. It has the character of an old newsreel from World War Two. The camera is jerky, the action speedy and contrived. There is no sound. There is a grainy, sepia quality to the film. Scenes are etched with abrasions, stains, scratches and splices.

The flickering light and the staccato clicking of the 16mm have a hypnotic, nostalgic effect on Gerald. He feels his pain subside. He allows himself to relax, to drop his guard.

The first scenes are wide-angle shots of the estate as it was in its heyday. Vast colonial-style mansion. White-washed walls. Spanish roof tiles. Portals and a large central patio. Wrought iron chairs with cushions. Wrought iron tables with glass tops. Balconies with hanging plants, hammocks, wicker loveseats. Tall windows with shutters. Massive carved wooden doors.

The grounds are a gridwork of lawns, flower gardens, and hedgerows. Aisles of palm trees bearing coconuts. Tennis courts. Swimming pool with Japanese footbridge spanning its width. Gazebo with thatched palm roof.

The jungle mass outside the complex extends for miles and miles towards a volcanic cordillera on the horizon. In a grassy clearing a uniformed man sits in a jeep with rigid posture, his hands on the steering wheel. A DC-3 approaches over the tops of the trees. It lands in the clearing. The man drives the jeep out to the plane. The door of the plane opens. A step ladder is lowered. A stocky man in a gaudy uniform walks down the steps. His chest is festooned with ribbons, medals, and tassels that quiver from his epaulettes. He waves at the camera.

The estate grounds are filled with people. Men and women sit on balconies talking, gesturing, holding drinks in their hands.

Women in bathing suits lie on mats around the swimming pool.

On the patio a party is in full swing. People talk in small groups. Some dance. A dozen men and women are gathered and singing boisterously around an upright piano.

In the gazebo a serious discussion is taking place. Men, some in uniform and some in business suits, shake their heads, gesticulate wildly, propose a toast.

Armed guards pace the perimeter.

At the beach, ramadas stand between water and jungle. Beneath one of them a man and a woman lounge together in a hammock. They smile for the camera.

Bare-chested men in swimming trunks pursue a woman in a petticoat along the beach. They catch up to her, lift her over their heads, dash out into the water. In a coordinated move they balance the woman in their uplifted arms, then toss her like a battering ram into an oncoming wave.

Generals arrive at the estate in jeeps. Many ceremonials. Many salutes, some in the Nazi manner.

Gala inside. Majestic ballroom with crystal chandeliers. Uniforms. Low-cut gowns. A woman on top of the piano, legs crossed, drink in one hand, cigarette in the other—.

The film broke with a loud snap.

Mercedes let out a curse in some language Gerald could not understand.

"Oh, that always happens," she said, screwing the lightbulb back on. "These films are pretty old, pretty brittle. It was almost over anyway. I hope you found it of some interest. I've got one other little film—one more gift—for you."

Mercedes kept talking as she unraveled the broken film from the projector.

"There's a whole film archive from the grand old days. Some of the movies are similar to what we just watched. A lot of them are commercial stag films, some real raunchy stuff. Then there's some Hollywood classics. Some Mexican films, too. They kept all the reels in a locked closet. For some reason the hurricane spared them. I've been through most of it. Historically it's quite interesting. You'd be amazed at who used to show up at this place."

Nothing, Gerald thought, would surprise me about this unreal place.

A bag of popcorn appeared in front of his face. He felt no alarm. He felt only an acute appetite for popcorn.

Mercedes stood with her back to Gerald as she threaded the next film.

He reached out, clutching the bag of popcorn with one hand and a girl's arm with the other. He pivoted his body and saw the girl standing behind the settee. Amanda. She wore a tentative smile on her face, a trace of fear. With her free hand she put a finger to her lips, signaling him to be quiet, to keep the secret. He gave her a wink and let go of her arm. She slipped away into the darkness.

Mercedes had the movie ready to go. She turned, looked at Gerald, looked at the popcorn in his lap.

Inexplicably, Gerald felt a sweet guilt. He felt like a child who tried to get away with something and got caught.

"I, uh . . . I was just. . . I. . . ."

"Never mind," said Mercedes. "That girl! She can't resist a good joke."

Laughing, Mercedes put the light out again and rolled the film.

FILM IN COLOR

A flat-bed diesel with four men in the cab rolls along a rough jungle road. On the front of the truck are the painted words "El Terror del Bosque."

The battered vehicle comes to a clearing, drives over an expanse of sand and rubble, drives up to the main entrance of the ruin.

The men get out of the truck. Amanda runs out to greet them. They talk. She goes back inside, comes out again with Mercedes.

The men take their hats off. They talk for a time with Mercedes. She gestures towards one end of the estate. They get back in the truck and drive to where she pointed.

The men carefully lower the body off the truck bed. They carry the filthy sleeping man across a threshold, into a roofless enclosure. They clear a space for him on the sandy floor. They put a blanket over him and leave.

Misha ambles over the ruins of the tennis courts. Nonchalantly the beige cow makes her way over the sand and succulents. She nibbles on a bush here and there. She passes over an arched bridge with rusted wrought iron dragons. She arrives at the room where the villagers have put the man.

Misha peeks into the doorway. She flutters her fin-like ears.

Pelicans and an iguana are perched on top of the jagged, vine-laden walls.

The man inside is stirring. He gropes about on the sand. He vomits on himself. His pants are soiled.

Misha enters the room, curious. She lowers her nose, close to the man. She sniffs him, steps away from him. She browses on shrubs that grow out of broken tiles.

The man rolls around violently on the ground. He makes several awkward attempts to catch hold of Misha's tail.

Finally he succeeds. Misha arches up, terrified. She kicks out her hind legs, barely missing the man's head. She frantically drags him around the room over tiles, brush, vines.

The birds ascend. The iguana flees.

Out the door and into the jungle, Misha runs full bore, pulling the man behind her. In her fright she defecates on him.

The cow and the man disappear into the green world.

Mercedes sweats as she hefts the blade. She wipes her brow. With the handle she draws her hair back. She hacks her way into the bush with the razor sharp machete. Amanda follows close behind her. They create a pathway to the man.

He is face down, unconscious. They stare at him, then return to the ruin.

Amanda goes to look for Misha.

Mercedes, with great effort, lugs a heavy plank out to the man in the jungle. She fetches a hemp rope. She sets the plank alongside the man. She rolls his body over, onto the board. With the rope she binds him to it.

Amanda returns, leading the beige cow.

With the slack in the rope Mercedes ties the makeshift litter to the cow.

Misha pulls the man, feet-first, from the place she had taken him. She pulls him across the grounds, the bridge, the tennis courts, to the path leading to the sea.

Men and women from the village walk along the beach. They stop to look at the man. Bound to the board, hitched to the cow, he continues to sleep.

Children arrive. Amanda gathers them. Proudly, she shows them the man.

Two fishing boats put ashore. The fishermen jump out and join the curious.

An old man plays a violin.

More villagers arrive, and a few campesinos.

A VW bug sputters up the beach. Two men in white shirts with badges get out.

A large crowd forms around the man and the beige cow. No one gets too close because of the smell. No one touches.

A guitarist arrives.

Mercedes brings a basket of refreshments from the house.

The sun sets into a distant fog bank on the horizon.

Women take fish from the boats. A pit is dug under a ramada. A fire is started.

People dance in the sand.

A man steps out of the jungle and approaches. He wears a straw bolo hat with long feathers in it.

Mercedes dances with the fishermen.

Children run along the beach. They set off firecrackers.

The sun breaks out again, brilliant between the water and the distant cloud. A woman crosses herself as it sets a second time.

Two dogs sniff at the stinking man on the plank. They fight. They tear into each other and tumble into the sand under Misha's tail.

The brahma, wide-eyed with fright, breaks for the sea.

The dancers step aside for the cow and the man in tow.

The dogs separate. They chase the man, frightening Misha all the more.

Mercedes attempts to stop Misha before she reaches the water.

Misha heads straight out to sea with the man behind her. Men jump headlong into the waves but she swims ahead of them.

The man on the plank remains unconscious, floating one moment, sinking the next.

The rope breaks.

Misha's head is still visible on the water, but the man is no longer seen. The villagers look for a sign of him. He is swept under the surface by the undertow.

The fishermen act quickly with their boats. Their knowledge of the water tells them where to go. One by one they dive from their boats, fanning out and sinking two large nets.

The people on shore help bring in the nets. The first yields only fish. The second has fish in abundance and the man.

The man is no longer bound to the plank. He is naked, a white mass folded inward in the prenatal position.

The people untangle him from the net. They carry him up to the dry sand, near the fire. He appears to be dead. The villagers gather around him, speechless. Mercedes drops to her knees.

The man with the feathered hat steps into the firelight. He kneels by the man on the ground, puts an ear to the man's chest, listens. He slaps the man, brutally hard, on the side of the head.

The beige cow is led from the sea by Amanda and the children.

The man coughs and chokes, vomits sea water, breathes.

The Healing Leaves

RAY GONZALEZ

As a boy my legs and arms ached
with growing pains.
My grandmother always pulled out
her bottle of rubbing alcohol,
a muddy brown oil full
of soaking leaves.

Strong smell of a healing aura
rose when she opened the green bottle,
tipped it in her large palms and
rubbed me down with the leaves,
black layers of wet skin,
glistening pieces of strong branches.

Overpowering plants fermented
in a bottle that held a dark swamp,
a fire that cured me as
hot hands traced the shape of leaves
across my trembling arms,
covered my legs like a small animal
found under the smoking trees.

The Pencil and the Scorpion

RAY GONZALEZ

I found the red scorpion crawling
up my bare foot and knew
it was time to die,
fresh out of high school
in the desert heat of June,
my bedroom in my parent's house
the only place I could
write my first poems,
the scorpion the only visitor
I had late at night.
I shook it off my foot with a pencil
and it sprang up the wall,
then landed on the window screen.
I turned off the lamp
to light a candle,
its glow spreading to the scorpion.

I stepped closer and watched it become
a red teardrop on the window,
bloodstain of a long future
of writing poems,
its erect tail poised
to sting at the clear vision
I only had back then,
at the age of seventeen,
the power of the scorpion
I touched with the pencil,
the flash of red I saw
for one brief moment
I would never capture, again,
in twenty years of writing.

I went back to my desk
in the candle light,
sat barefoot and waited
for the morning to hide
all its creatures,
waited for the sting at the heart
that wears down our pencils,
decade after decade of scorpions
hiding under the bed,
pencil after pencil leaving
red marks like baby scorpions crawling
over their mother's back.

Was Federico Garcia Lorca Lonely in New York?

RAY GONZALEZ

Was Federico Garcia Lorca lonely in New York?
Did he climb the streets like a statue of rock
rebelling against the sculptor, turning on
his creator to take the chisel out of his hands?

Was Federico crying in New York?
Did he wipe his tears with hands borne of oranges
whose juice punishes all men of crippled hope,
or did he stare at the harbor and wait for the gulls
to screech into blinding stars shooting across
immigration lines, bread lines of people
too hungry to drink their cups of blood?

Was Garcia Lorca able to sleep in New York?
Did he wake above the city blocks to identify
the makers of brick and mortar, builders of slums,
ghosts of abandoned rooms, doors of troubled sleep?

Did Lorca slash the *duende* in New York?
Did he find the black guitar in the ashes
raining over the Brooklyn Bridge,
or meet the many-colored gypsy in the alley
of singing flames, the barrio of wailing love
and the forgotten tambourine?

Was Federico searching for something in New York?
Did Spain turn into a wolf hunting for him
as he looked for the woman of flowers in Central Park,
search for the child in the fish markets of Harlem,
go after the crowds of people everywhere?

Did Garcia Lorca go crazy in New York?
Were his eyes drilling the heart of the subways
to find a place to hide his poems?
Before leaving, did he dance the step of death in recognition
of firing squads lining up in every country?

Did Lorca run toward the lights
of the harbor of false liberty?
Did he finally get out of the way,
or was he carried to the moon by the thousands
of pigeons fleeing the future city?

The National Geographic World Atlas

JOEL FRIEDERICH

My father would hand it down to me, saying, "Be careful, this is heavy," the great red book, wide enough to be my bed. I turned the pages of the world with two hands: the magnitude of stars and the crystalline structure of topaz, cirrostratus and cumulo-nimbus, silver landscapes of the moon and exploding volcanoes and blue ocean bottoms with mountains so clear, I tried to touch edges and hollows that weren't there. I saw the earth split open like an apple; I could curl up and sleep on its pages with my head on the Himalayas.

In August my mother ran like mad getting ready and my father fastened the carrier to the top of the car. By brother and I stared at the blue and red veins of Wisconsin tracing with our fingers and trying to imagine what it would be like when we got there: the musty cabin, long watery days, children with strange languages, and nights: laughter and silence and music hanging forever on the lake while we lay breathing and aware in beds that were not our own. I began to see this in the book and crept downstairs at night to stare at other states.

When they came, it was before dawn and I was not asleep, listening to my brother's dream and watching the darkness congeal into continents and stars and oceans of night. My brother began to cry when they lifted him in their arms wrapped in blankets, and I saw how small he was. I held my mother's hand and walked outside to the car, surprised by the chill of the air in August. I had never seen a night so enormous, so quiet and aware. We were going, we were thieves and we were travelers, and no one knew it but us, moving carefully through the dark, waking no one. I looked at my father holding his bundle of sobs and he nodded his head to me as if to say, "Be careful, this is heavy," and he handed my brother down into the car.

As we moved out through the streets his head fell on my lap and I saw all the roads and rivers untangling from the page. I slept in the motion of the world moving past.

The Mountains to the South

JOEL FRIEDERICH

One day my lover comes to me and says that she is going. I hear winds blowing across ridges and enormous wings beating through branches. When she repeats my name, it is the sound of a stone clattering down bright canyon walls.

I begin to forget immediately.

When she has gone, I go out and look at the mountains to the south. I remember her face in the summer rain, her arms resting on dry grass in the fall, her hair falling down white forests of winter.

I am looking at fading colors, diminishing shapes.

I cannot hold my death like a little yellow bird in my palm. It has the depth of many ranges behind the sun, the sadness of many hues in the wounded sky. It flees before me as I walk toward it.

I alter my memory through this moment of looking.

Once, behind a night club, I saw two lovers struggle in the darkness. I am born this moment with storms about my head and lightning in my mouth; with a dozen darkening ranges and a separate birth on each black peak.

Asthmatics

PETER WILD

Eating a moth, the praying mantis
trembles, in his mouth a winged letter
        from God, a man with the palsy
shaken at the feast of himself.

So I have seen children in schoolyards
                        around the world
waving sheer sashes, swinging their legs to heaven
as they walk, calling out to a cloud,
        a big dog floating over,
even those without socks in their mouths
Jansenists all.

We hear that in Japan
            as the economy grows
faster than their grand parents ever imagined
teenagers are rushing into marriage
            by the tens of thousands;
love will make them immortal.

You thought he was the archfiend
            come to get you
when as a girl in New Jersey
you first saw him on your bedroom wall,

And like any asthmatic cried out
until, catching the air,
        you slept well with your mother,
    and your father lay in your place
for years, unconvinced, still an alcoholic.

Travel Agents

PETER WILD

The archfiend is turned loose in the sky,
speeding on the wings of her own power,
for the wind through her pinions whistles
like a man who hears what's in
      his phylacteries speaking to him
and needs no other guide but swoops
and darts overjoyed by his own shadow
flashing beneath him across the earth and buoyed
on the adrenaline of his own music.
And what can we do about it
as she sweeps by and we down here
      stand dumbly pointing our fescues?
On street corners our children see
cops who've been mostly honest,
         who've been thinking of retirement,
of spending their last years, grown wise,
         fishing through the ice,
collapse with their first but final moans
as she goes over like balloons
with the air all at once let out of them,
while out in the fields graduates of MIT
are marshalling phalanxes of fire trucks,
      but even as they scheme the wheat
around them, their very hair, turn white, catch fire,
and they begin to dance like men seeing the future,
in which their wives leave them to become travel agents.

His City

CHRISTOPHER WOODS

Coming up the road in that sad region, he thought he recognized a tree. First one, then another, along that road. Finally he recognized an entire line of trees, and he remembered having helped plant them, many years before. It came to him that he had been away a long time, perhaps thirty years if the trees could be trusted. They were mere saplings when he left.

Doubtless this city, Bastillo, had changed greatly. Other men his age had married, had fathered children. His former friends had worked alongside each other in this city, the one he never had believed was his own. He had banished himself from it. The only things he had touched, it seemed, were the trees, and they didn't recognize him. He was thinking about this, how nothing seemed to belong to him, when he came into the city.

Maybe some of his friends were already dead, he didn't know. Maybe buried outside the city in the ground he had thought too dusty. His city would be sturdy, built on rocky terrain. His city, he was sure, would not be built on a dusty plain in such a sad region. Not his city.

No one he passed in the street paid him much mind. Certainly no one recognized him. He realized that he would have a hard time recognizing someone he used to know. After all, by now he was much more familiar with the faces in his own city. Could he be expected to remember all these faces, and from so long ago? Then too, a fact remained. The people in this city were the stuff of someone else's dream.

So it came as something of a surprise when a woman he passed in the square stopped and stared. After a long moment she burst into tears and put her arms around him. An old woman, eightyish, dressed poor in yellowed muslin, with eyes as sad as the land itself.

Very gently, careful not to frighten the woman, he pushed her to the side to be free of her. If it was still there, he was thinking, there was a house he wanted to see. He set out for the street that led to that house. But so many streets, maybe a hundred more than he remembered, and soon he felt as though he was merely wandering.

Even if the woman was following him, even if she kept crying out so mournfully, he would not stop. He would not slow, or turn to look at her again. He ignored her cries, and would not admit he was her son. It was someone else's dream, even being born here, he knew. It was a brittle kind of knowledge that could confuse him if left to fester. He began walking faster, leaving the old crying woman behind.

He did not find that house that first afternoon. There was not time before the sun went down. Some things had not changed. No electricity in the city, just as he remembered. His city had electricity. It had running water. His city was never without ample food and drink. His city was not in a sad region.

It was dark, a deathly kind of night. He didn't know where he was going. When he stopped walking, he was at the bank of a river. He could feel the breeze off the water and smell the muddy shore, but the darkness hid the river itself. And he smelled food being cooked somewhere close, down the darkness of the bank.

They took him in, a small band of workers who would sleep on a bluff overlooking the unseen water flow. If they recognized him, they didn't let on. In the dark, listening to their voices, he realized they were young enough to be his sons. They didn't ask him where he was coming from, or where he was going. But he asked for some work, he didn't care what, and that made them accept him. They gave him food, and a blanket. Maybe he'd be one of their own kind, that's all they could have thought.

In his city, he had decided, there would not be such a thing as hard work. It only meant that all the people who had come before, who had worked the centuries through, had worked in vain. They hadn't been able to get rid of it, of work. All they did was work toward something, but no one seemed to know what. It just kept going on. Going on.

Of course he didn't tell the others about his city, and the fact of little work. Such a thing would make them edgy, and perhaps suspicious. He didn't complain how exhausted he was by the next afternoon, when the cargo loading was done. They had laden a small steamship with what appeared to be some kind of native product in large crates. He didn't know what it was he struggled with all day. All he knew was that the cargo smelled half of tar and half of dust, and that it was going somewhere else.

After the work was complete the workers headed for the place on the bluff again. He walked slowly, letting them get ahead of him. By the time they reached the bluff he was nowhere to be seen, by any of them.

There was still that house he needed to find. The Bastillo house.

Bastillo had been the first to come along and set up camp on the dusty plain. He collected other people, he had the talent. Others, passing through the sad region, stayed for good. A city came from nothing but dust and the river's lifeblood. Bastillo named the town after himself.

It was Bastillo's house he was looking for, street after changed street, in the final daylight. Once darkness took hold, he groped his way, house after house. An hour passed, maybe two. He talked to no one as few were outside. They were sleeping, passing time until the work business started up again. Started up again.

He was lucky. He could barely see his hand in front of his face, but he caught sight of the gables on the Bastillo house. The gables shone in a faint moonlight. The roof itself was so steep that it appeared to pierce the moon. A house like this is not so hard to remember, he thought. And it was exactly as he remembered it, as he had hated it for some long years.

He unlatched the gate and walked directly below the great veranda of the house. The stairs did not moan when his weight shifted from one step to the next. Standing at the door, he thought about all the time he had been away, and how far he had walked. And how much hate played a part, how it had propelled him to return.

Then he spat on the door and the beveled windows. He spat on the chairs and tables that graced the veranda. Then, when his mouth was dry, he retraced his steps back down the stairs to the gate. He went back as he had come, street after street, until he reached the edge of the city. The farther away from the city he got, the more he felt the sadness of the plain lifting. The air cleared, in his mind.

In time it would be clear enough that he would know the place for his city when he came to it. Bastillo had found his during a flood, when his boat capsized. He swam ashore first, before anyone else. The tide gave him a city to call his own. One man's city could not become another's, so the logic went.

So he knew his city was something to be certain of, nearer or farther on the road, or in a storm, or sometimes as they come, in a dream. He felt that his city would come in the latter fashion. He slept much, and dreamed much. In his city, with no work to steal his time, he could sleep and dream as much as he pleased.

But his sleep was anxious. He was in a hurry for a voice to come to him and direct him to his city. He was getting older. These trips to other cities from which he had been banished aged him greatly. His memory was going with age. It became a problem, remembering which city he had already traveled to, all the houses he had spat at. All he could do was keep on. Keep on.

Zeros in Mine

ANTHONY WALLACE

One day she just ached into being, asked for money. I barked until I knew the story. When she talks, the cows in the pasture graze into memory. Nostrils police the air, so I couldn't change the channel. But she wanted more lies than I could give her. The need of the only outweighs the need.

I live alone with others. Everyone comes from a debatable household, broken by unity. But salt water runs in her family. So the nuns in the church tuck their shirt-tails in. There was nowhere to go, since my torso wingless. At the altar, we use exact change.

Stomping with Pettit on the Battenkill

GARRETT KAORU HONGO

I need to whoop it up some
   and drive fast on the highways
singing to Ronstadt and Hank Williams
   loud on the tinny car stereo,
screaming like Little Richard as we whoosh by
   the roadside maples and birches,
slide-wheeling around the curves,
   ignoring all the sunburnt flag-ladies
as they try to stop us or slow us down.

I need to smoke sweet Jamaican cigars,
   puffing like an old steam engine,
screaming to the ponds and the Saabs
   and the covered bridges,
and waving at the white fronds of nimbus clouds
   passing us overhead.

I need to celebrate the first day of summer fishing
   and the easy birth of your son
and your Polaroid pictures from the hospital,
   his moist eyes and pink skin and Dara
in her gown and glamourously matted hair,
   and you in your green scrub suit
and Guy in his white cotton cap
   and his amazement.

I need to swoop down from the clouds and the antenna
   like a fat and looney bird
full of zip and Chinese food
   and great powers of exaggeration
and see water rushing over freestone beds,
   churning in frothy riffles

and languishing in green pools deep with promise
   and heavy with cannibal fish.

I need to march by a field of singing corn
   and recite Roethke and Donne and Yeats
and rave on thrashing through underbrush,
   hopping puddles and sliding down
muddy banks over slippery rock
   and wading in and feeling the cool, bronze water
press in around me, sensing the current
   washing me down to the New York line.

It's necessary to exhaust myself
   and trudge back to your truck,
fall asleep in the cab with the doors open
   and my feet sticking out
with my boots and waders still on,
   and dream about Ishmael and Agamemnon,
about Montana and the miracles of Elizabeth Bishop
   and a moose trailing us on the Henry's Fork.

I need to wake with mosquitoes humming in my ears
   and the *plink* and *pop* of trout rising
in the slick water of the pool below,
   and think about Horace
and the pleasures of country life,
   and hear the slap of your line on flat water
and the hogcalls and hoots of pleasure you make
   as if you were just born.

The Disciple

MELISSA MILLER

I

Blue tattoo
on his belly,
yin and yang engraved
over solar plexus
home of ki,
he declares himself
the child of balance.

If you poised him
on a pencil
at that spot
he wouldn't tip.

If you tied a rope there and pulled
he would fly symmetrically,
his legs and head
bending back
forming a crescent moon.

If you stabbed him
right there
death
would reach both ends
at the same time.

A kiss
would reach his heart
and groin
together.

II

A scroll
tattooed across the sign—
empty . . .
he waits.

He will surf
the blue water
until he breaks
into molecules.

He will sit
under a tree
until roots
wrap around him.

He will climb
a mountain
until ice
claims him.

He will stare
at a flame
until light
consumes him.

He waits until
words find him.

Lightning Stork

SUSAN BARNETT

"It is no myth,
the Lightning Stork,"
the chief Kikuyu says,
wearing his pride like a feather cloak,
draped easy over bony shoulders.

"All over East Africa,"
his arm sweeps wide,
"the Lightning Stork is known.
He calls the lightning from the sky;
the gods do his bidding."

I nod, smile politely,
unaware he's read my upturned brow
until he searches my eyes,
bursts into a gap-toothed grin,
wags a finger at the sky
as if to teach a lesson

Then night, outside my tent,
I ponder the experience
of shimmering land and luminescent sky;
remember his echoing laughter still
like music in this quiet place—
What was he searching for my eyes?

I hear a rustling in the bush,
study the shadows, animal-shaped,
then suddenly see a giant stork
bathed in the spotlight of the moon

Balanced on one straw leg,
it lifts its pointed beak,
scans the whirling sky,
screams a high familiar cry
that echoes pain too harsh for human ears—
a yowling, bawling, screeching stork,
piercing the listening night

Then comes the rain,
quenching the dry land;
then comes the lightning,
jagged spears;
then comes the thunder's
distant rumbling,
voices of the answering gods'
ancient Illumination:

After Bird Watching Near the Mexican Border

ROBERT BURLINGAME

I am slow moving.
Like Mexico, the land we walk next to.
But we're not, in truth, lazy. I gaze west, south.
Mexico, always.
I feel passionate music grip my thighs. I sing.
I feel purposeful as milk in a summer breast.

All morning, in this bosque, we watched birds.
Birds irreverently flying across the uniformed border,
ruled line guarded by balloons, patrols, or by
worms with eyes hidden in their genitals:

   Painted bunting, yellow billed cuckoo, burrowing owl,
grackel, air-widening swift, small finch. We watched them,
elegant trespassers of man's ignorance.
We drank from our canteens. A heron flew crazily into Mexico,
Mexico—white wall beneath the shadows of ascension.

Birds dovetailed, broke apart in a scattering of seconds;
vivid as women at the moment of spasm, they delivered
themselves from the green caves of June.
We are denied their adventure. We must imagine.
  So tell me, my friend, where is the woman with our coffee,
  that one with a smile like a deliberate, slow wing?

Reply to a Dull Photograph of Chekhov

ROBERT BURLINGAME

Chekhov in his Victorian clothes
is a suit of clothes,
insipidly victorian. He is
not a writer, not Vanka's most
tender overlooker, not the Darling's
ultimate spouse at home
in an opinionless grove of lindens.

Chekhov in his starched collar,
his sharp bow tie, is hardly Chekhov at all.
He is dressed in the drabness he loathed—
poshlust. Even the wicker chair he sits
in is as stupid as a Tartar's knout.

But his right hand draped musingly
over the chair's arm is charged with
Apollo's thunder, with Dionysus's
joy stupendous against the haughtiness
of mountain ivy. It tells the story:

Chekhov, rising,
will stagger through the pillared ballroom,
he'll howl the names he loved: Zhenya,
Nikanor, Pyotor, Semyon, Kastanka.
We'd see him then, his hands reaching,
his coat gone, the tie dangling.
We'd see him—dervish of old Russia.

Las Cruces and Five Lost Years
for Doug Bedell

ALBINO CARILLO

When you climbed
into the middle of April
as you did, sure of grip,
were you afraid like me,
afraid sometimes
to ease from bed,
pull on shoes, a soiled shirt?
Because of you
I wonder what will be
my final picture.

Once, crossing a swollen river,
I worried and slipped.
I recall two bees,
awash as I was,
golden in their struggle.
And that's all:
Afterward, I carried my wet clothes,
my soaked shoes, as testament.
Clinging to that rock,
I have you,
in my mind, admiring
the texture of sandstone.

As a child,
my father climbed
the Organ Mountains:
If I believe him,
he went to see the sun,
said he could see his house,
feel his mother's angry shouts.
Scrambling over the ridge
as he probably did,
as you did, years later,
mistakes are easy;
the desire to touch the rocks,
again and again,
grows each day, each hour.

Black and White

CARLOS NICOLAS FLORES

As he walked into the shadows cast by the lush trees overreaching the driveway, he saw the shadow (although he knew it couldn't have been a shadow because it was too black and its outline too finely etched for a shadow), or a shawl (although he knew it couldn't be that either because it was too round, full and furry), or a black mink stole (but what would a mink stole be doing lying in the dirt at the edge of the driveway?). It stood up on four legs; a tail curled in the air. A black cat. It was an ordinary black cat. And it crossed his path.

Américo balked. Bad luck, he surmised. What would it be this time? That he had overdrawn his account at the bank and would be left without funds the rest of the month? Perhaps something as commonplace but devastating as an attractive woman's rejection in some squalid nightclub? A jealous ex-husband coming after him with a .38? Or a car wreck like the one in which a student of his died two months ago? Was there nothing to do now, in an absurd world, except wait for something to leap out of the bushes and maul him?

The black cat paused and glanced back at him, then darted behind the house.

As he came to his senses, he looked about to see if anyone had seen him. What would people think if they knew he had just been cowed by an ordinary black cat? He shook his head, moved on, and unlocked the door to his apartment.

In the kitchen, first one, then another orange lizard raised its head from among the dirty dishes and grease-thick black skillet in the sink. They cocked their heads and stared at Américo. Odors from rancid food and stale beer hung heavily in the air. It was Sunday, and he still had not washed Friday's dishes. What would Dagoberto, clean and fastidious as he was, think if he knew that every weekend he was away, lizards inhabited the dishes on which he ate? Not bad luck, Américo concluded, but a chaotic life, which breeds all sorts of ills—that's what's wrong with me. He got to work.

After he dispatched the lizards and washed the dishes, he swept the apartment, then mopped it. When he gazed at the gleaming floor, he felt as if he had removed every spot where a threat to his equanimity might hide.

Outside, a car door slammed shut. Dagoberto, no doubt. Relieved that he would not have to apologize for a mess this time, Américo walked to the refrigerator and took out a cold beer.

The front door opened. Dagoberto walked in and flashed a lively grin at Américo. "Hi."

Américo sat down at the table. "How did it go in San Antonio?"

Dagoberto put his briefcase on the table. "We had a wonderful time." He laid his clothes over the back of a chair in the living room, then returned to the kitchen. "My parents came up from the valley. My brother and I took them out to eat. I ran across an old friend from my seminary days. When he saw Blanca, he finally understood why I had to leave the seminary."

The photos of Dagoberto's fiancée, an elegantly svelte woman with a sharply angled beautiful face, large green eyes and blonde hair, had impressed a mateless Américo.

Dagoberto opened the refrigerator door, took out some ham and bread, and began preparing himself a sandwich on the kitchen counter. "I found the car I've been looking for, a four door sedan, new, good price. It'll be easier to drive my parents around. They're old. They have a hard time getting in and out of the coupe." He glanced at Américo. "Have you ever thought about getting rid of that heap you drive around in and buying a new car?"

Américo looked sharply at Dagoberto, "Do you know how much I'm spending on my psychiatrist?"

Dagoberto took a beer out of the refrigerator. "A lot, probably."

Américo waited for his roommate to sit down at the table. "In three years you'll have an aging car, and hopefully I'll have a new life."

Dagoberto gave his friend a doubtful look and said nothing. Instead, he crossed himself and began to pray over his food. Américo waited. He hated priests, nuns, and Catholics, a prejudice he had inherited from his father. He wondered what the hell he was doing rooming with an erstwhile priest.

As soon as Dagoberto finished, Américo rose and went to his bedroom. He heard Dagoberto turn on the television in the kitchen. The six o'clock news came on. Américo went in the bathroom and showered. When he returned to his room, he took a clean set of clothes from the closet and began dressing. He didn't look forward to working in his office that evening, but he had to grade a stack of papers before class the next morning.

"Come look at this," said Dagoberto from the kitchen.

Américo walked to the kitchen. The scenes of soldiers carrying wounded men on stretchers left him cold. He returned to his bedroom at once, bitter memories of his three months in the army threatening to upset him. His brother, Johnny, had just returned from Vietnam several months before, a wreck. From what Américo could gather, the Americans were in trouble. I'm through with all that, he thought with rancor. It was never my war anyway.

The phone rang. Dagoberto answered it. "It's for you. Long distance."

Américo went to the kitchen and took the phone. The operator turned the call over to the speaker at the other end, whose familiar voice Américo recognized at once. "Mavaro, how are you? What's up?"

"I've got bad news." Mavaro paused. "Johnny is dead."

"What?"

"He was killed in a car accident."

The wail of the bereaved pierced Américo's ear. It was his mother. "Hijo de mi vida, Johnny! Why did you leave me? Oh, Johnny!"

"Let me speak to her!"

"She'll be all right. Just come quickly."

"Let me talk to Pop!"

"He can't right now. He's with Mom. How long will you be?"

"I . . . I don't know."

He put the receiver back on the wall. In its wake reigned a silence such as Américo had never known before, assertive and unlimited. A strange change overcame him as he sat down at the kitchen table. Américo felt the same outrage and perplexity he had felt the time a neighborhood friend threw Johnny down on a pile of cinderblocks; he had cut his head, and it bled profusely. Américo had picked up his BB gun and, stopping in the middle of the alley, fired at the fleeing boy.

"Fucking asshole," he muttered. "Just like Johnny to go kill himself."

Dagoberto lowered the volume of the television. "What's the matter?"

Américo looked up. "My brother just killed himself." He realized what he had said and corrected himself. "I mean he got killed in an auto accident."

Dagoberto approached Américo. "I'm very sorry to hear that."

Américo rose. "It's no big deal! The sonuvabitch deserved it! Now everybody can rest!"

Dagoberto, taken aback by something he had never seen before, stared at Américo. Américo changed his tone of voice, "I didn't mean to speak to you that way. It's just that . . . it's something I've known would happen sooner or later."

"Is there anything I can do?"

Américo thought of all the things he had to attend to now. "I'll need a ride to the airport tomorrow."

As the airplane began its descent over the familiar disjunction between mountains and desert, Américo sat up and glued his face to the porthole. The landscape of West Texas was so dramatically different from that of South Texas. West Texas let him open up and reach for the heights of the mountains; in South Texas, he felt encroached upon by the chaparral, kept close to the earth.

As he got off the plane, Américo felt queasy. To his great surprise, he calmed down when he saw the somber, injured faces of his brother and father. He embraced his father, who held him a long time and wept.

When Américo climbed inside his father's pickup truck and sat between Mavaro and the door, he took a deep breath of anticipation. It would be a long drive home. The mountains ahead and the vast sky above them brought Johnny to mind. They had climbed those mountains together.

At the house everything was exactly the way it had been the last time Américo was there—the sidewalk, the white walls, the roof aglitter with rocks, the rocking chairs on the porch, the black metal door. In the living room his little brother and sisters scampered from the kitchen and embraced him. The mixture of delight and hurt in their young faces touched him; he kissed and hugged them with feeling. He followed his father to the bedroom where his mother, her face tear-stained and fatigued from grief, got to her feet and touched his face as if relieved to see she had not lost another child.

Américo held this short, stocky woman whose hair was as black as his.

"Oh, Américo," she cried, "Johnny is dead!"

"Yeah, Mom, I know," was all he could offer. But he spoke softly.

As she pressed her face against his chest, which muffled her crying, he was surprised to find himself reacting with such poise—finding, in fact, the role of comforter familiar and welcome. He had always been considered the strongest one in the family.

At last she let go of him and wiped her eyes. "I'll make you something to eat."

"I'm not hungry, Mom. Thanks. Why don't you get some rest?"

"No, no," she set out for the kitchen, "I've already taken the meat out of the refrigerator."

He relented. "I'll be on the porch outside with Mavaro. Call me when the food is ready."

Señor Izquierdo, a short man with an intense face and small energetic eyes, stopped Américo on his way to the living room. "Is there anything you need from the store? Some milk, fruit?"

Milk and fruit were the last things Américo wanted under the circumstances. Why couldn't his father ever offer anything more appropriate? "No, thanks, Pop. I need to talk to Mavaro."

Américo draped his coat on the back of the sofa and walked outside to the porch where Mavaro joined him on the metal rocking chairs.

The gigantic series of triangles produced by the mountains slanting upon the blue sky engaged Américo's attention. There had been a time he could sit in that chair and gaze at the mountains for hours.

He turned to Mavaro, whose shy narrow, dark face he had always liked. "So what happened?"

"You know how he was before you left."

Boy, did he. Johnny seemed like a caged animal. Every night, reeking of liquor, he banged his way to his old bedroom; every night Señor Izquierdo, a towel held about his naked body with one hand, sallied from his bedroom and confronted Johnny in a tumult of futile scoldings. Every day at noon Johnny unlocked the bedroom door and disappeared on the pretext that he was looking seriously for a job, which he never found.

Mavaro went on, "We were home when we got a telephone call. It was the police. They said a man fitting Johnny's description had just been killed in an auto accident. They needed a relative to identify him. So I drove out there. It was him all right, lying there as if he had just fallen off the mountain. That was the easy part. Having to drive back here to tell everybody was tough."

Américo imagined Mavaro walking into the living room, where the family had assembled, and delivering the dreadful news. Somehow Américo felt he should have been there. But, no, he was glad he hadn't been and admired Mavaro for handling the situation by himself.

"I talked to his girl friend," Mavaro said. "He called her before he left the bar where he was playing pool. He was going to pick her up at work. She said he sounded stoned and drunk. She tried to dissuade him. But you know Johnny. He drove all the way from South El Paso, coming up on Alabama. Just past the turn into McKelligon Canyon, he hit a curve. He was going too fast. The convertible flew off the road and flipped. He was thrown. His body was pierced by yucca daggers."

Américo winced. Once in the mountains he stumbled on a yucca dagger. It hurt like hell.

"That's not what killed him. The impact broke his neck. He died instantly."

Mavaro fell silent. Américo's eyes returned to the mountains. He had missed them. They were the same ones, so magnificent, he had contemplated as a child when his family first moved to this suburb in the northeastern part of town. His gaze focused on the peak in the distance. They had called it Sugar Loaf. The road along which Johnny had been travelling skirted its base. Américo knew the exact place where Johnny had been killed. Many times Johnny, Américo, and their friends had crossed the road at the point where it curved in order to reach the arroyos. Sweating in the blazing sun, their mouths parched, with knapsacks on their backs and canteens on their waists, he and Johnny led their gang of friends up the cacti-infested slopes. For self-defense against imagined enemies, they carried the BB guns their mother had bought them and wore the army helmets they had painted white. At the top of the peak they discovered a metal shed-like construction, which at one time might have been a radio relay station or perhaps a beacon. There they quenched their thirst as they looked at the valley's desert floor stretching to the next mountain range. The cooling breeze and the silence had been delightful. He remembered Johnny as an excellent climber. On the mountains, which had devoured several GI's from the base, he could be trusted.

"Well," said Américo, as he beheld Mavaro, "this was bound to happen sooner or later. He was in pretty bad shape when he got back. An army doctor told him he didn't have much longer to live. His liver was a mess. Remember the time he got sick?"

Mavaro nodded. "I remember. You got pissed off at the doctor for charging Pop so much for his house call."

"Those bastards—though the doctor did spot his swollen liver. Johnny told me that in 'Nam he'd been drinking a case of beer a day."

"Did you know about his wife?"

"The bitch from Florida?"

"No, the one in Vietnam. She's going to have a baby."

"No—Mom didn't tell me anything about her."

"The letter arrived yesterday."

"So now we have a nephew in Vietnam. Wouldn't it be strange if we met him one day and found out he looked just like Johnny?"

Mavaro shrugged his shoulders in bewilderment.

"What about the gringa from Florida?" asked Américo. "Has she written?"

"No. All I know is they never got divorced. It was one of the things he wanted to take care of as soon as he got back."

"Did he have any plans of bringing the Vietnamese over?"

"No."

"It figures."

The hefty Anglo-American woman had seemed twice Johnny's height and girth. Américo's initial suspicions when he first saw her walk in the front door of his parents' home were confirmed—the marriage would prove to be one more of the endless series of fiascos that had besieged the Izquierdo family. His mother, already dreaming about her new golden Anglo grandson, received the couple with open arms, convinced that a stint in the Air Force and now this spur-of-the-moment marriage would save her son. Sure enough, not one week after Johnny had absconded to Vietnam, his fat wife climbed on Johnny's resurrected ten-speed and headed for the nightclubs on the strip by the fort. More surprising to Américo was that his father, the man with an iron will and a face that would brook no opposition, took as long as he did to kick her out.

Américo spoke, "Is the funeral tomorrow morning?"

"Yes."

"Where is the rosary?"

Mavaro told him.

"Américo," the voice was his mother's, "your food is ready. Come and eat before it gets cold."

For a moment he felt like a child, being called by his mother after a long day of climbing the mountains. It seemed like just yesterday that he, Johnny, and their little gang of neighborhood friends had reached the summit of Mount Sugar Loaf for the first time. He recollected vividly a sensation that their lives, like the eternal mountains, would not change for a long time.

He stood up.

A slender girl with Indian black hair and a solemn brown face knelt at the casket and began crying quietly. Américo had seen her only in the photographs Johnny had shown him, but he recognized her; Johnny's girl friend from high school. Mavaro had claimed that, although she was divorced now and had a son, Johnny had expressed some interest in getting back together with her after his return. Américo never understood why Johnny left her for that fat gringa from Florida, but there were many things Américo didn't understand about his family.

More people stepped up to see Johnny, more than Américo had

expected to show up at the rosary that night. The Izquierdos, he knew, had never been close to anyone, not even to members of either his mother's or father's family. The sight of his Tio Escolastico standing in the line both surprised and pleased Américo; his mother's brother from Juarez had not set foot in the Izquierdos' home for years. Then he saw his Puerto Rican cousin, Salvador, a big, tall man with a red face and wavy blonde hair, whom Américo's father had brought to El Paso to live many years before. Salvador was followed by his Mexican wife and five children. Both Escolastico and Salvador had kept their distance from the Izquierdos because they distrusted his father. The friends who had shown up were mostly his father's, several salesmen and a lawyer. The rest Américo did not recognize.

The line thinned out. Deciding it was time, Américo arose and stood in line.

When his turn came, he knelt before the casket and beheld Johnny, his companion of the mountains. Johnny looked his best, just as Américo had remembered him—his black hair nicely combed, his large eyes in peaceful sleep, handsome. In his shiny coffin, Johnny was a far cry from the restless animal shipped back from Vietnam, his hair a mess, his face angry, putrescent, and wild-eyed. Seeing his brother under these circumstances proved easier than he had expected—no unruly emotions or frenzied tears.

The contusion, where his neck had snapped, was not ugly because the mortician had done a good cosmetic job.

—Fuck it!—It had been a favorite expression of Johnny's.

Américo remembered.

Johnny, looking up from where he sat watering the mimosa tree at their parents' house, smiled at Américo.

—Fuck it! I say. You can't let things get to you, Américo. Like that motherfucking sonavubitch of a master sergeant, Razzo the fatso asshole. Kept bugging me. Kept pushing me. Wouldn't get off my case. A big gringo. Thought he could push this little Mex around. I told myself I'm going to get this fucker. So I just watched him and waited. One day he comes yelling at the top of his voice, 'Izquierdo, you don't know your ass from a hole in the ground. You botched up that job.' I hadn't botched a damned thing. It had been those assholes working with me. So I just thought 'Fuck it!' I picked up a rubber mallet as big as that rock. When he went under the wing, I let him have it. Pow! Right on the noggin. You should have seen him go down. Cross-eyed, his tongue hanging out like a cow's. Fucker was lucky I didn't kill him.

The absolute stillness of Johnny's hands—brown and stubby, resting on his chest, positioned as if he were getting ready to pray—fascinated Américo.

—'Nam was a great party," Johnny continued, as he pushed back the sunglasses on his nose. "One night me and some guys decided to have a party. We were restricted to the base. So we packed the bunker at the airstrip with booze and pot and enough food to feed the whole V.C. army. Me—I took care of the women. Some fine Vietnamese women.

If Américo had envied Johnny anything, it had been his looks, the evenly shaped nose and lips, the compact form of his skull, and his sensual eyes. Johnny's style had been that of a duck-tailed, hip-swinging rock 'n' roll star. Américo didn't fully understand why he detested it, but he did, seeing it as an expression of a way of life he wanted no part of. Though he had envied Johnny's looks, he had felt nothing but contempt for the ineptitude—a hip, shallow irreverence—that had crushed his brother.

—Then the shelling began. You should see the craters those motherfuckers leave. The world was coming to an end when some asshole says, 'We forgot the ice!' How the hell can you party without ice? So I say, 'Fuck it!' I climbed out of the bunker. The earth shook so much I couldn't walk straight. My God, I had never seen such a good fireworks display. So I said, 'If I'm going to die it might as well be now because I'm not going to party without ice.' Boom! Boom! Nothing happened! I got the ice. I ran. Boom! Boom! The mothers weren't even close. Ha, ha!

—They didn't stop either. It went on all night. It was the party to end all parties. We danced, we laughed. I've never fucked so much. Those Vietnamese broads were great. They couldn't stand on their legs when we climbed out of the bunker. Anyway, to make a long story short, the next morning we found out the guys in the other bunkers had been hit. Wasted—all of them. Can you believe that? It just wasn't my time, dude. When my times comes, I plan to rock and roll my way to hell.

The howl, his mother's, came from above, not from behind him, reverberating from the ceiling where it cut the air in two, then struck Américo between the eyes. He turned to look at her. He couldn't see her face, shielded by his father's shoulder, just her black hair. She howled with all the pain, alien and discomfitting to Américo, that not even a woman giving birth must feel.

He looked at Johnny again. So this is it, he thought. This is what it all amounts to in the end. After all the denunciations and resentments and humiliations, you lie down and close your eyes not just for one night—but forever.

His eyes settled on his brother's face now swaddled in the coffin's satin oblivion. What do you say to a dead man? he wondered. Well, Johnny, he thought, I'll be seeing you around.

He stood up, reached into the coffin and touched Johnny's hand. It wasn't cold, as he had expected, just stiff and impersonal as hardened plaster of Paris.

A woman in high heels picked her way along the steep sidewalk towards Américo, a well-shaped figure in black with a dark veil across her face. She stopped. When she removed her veil, he recognized her once-beautiful face amid the splotches of ugly white that had disfigured her otherwise naturally brown skin. "Señora Obregon?"

"You do remember!" Her extraordinary voice—warm, melodious, and intelligent—evoked fond memories. "It's been such a long time, so many years. It's sad that we should see each other in such tragic circumstances. I read about the accident in the newspapers. Such a tragedy for your father and mother."

Américo nodded. "Thank you for coming. How's Alfredo?"

"Oh, Al got married and moved to Houston. He's doing very well there. I hope to join him soon."

A magnificent white angora cat arose in Américo's mind from the detritus of his bitter high school years. He recalled how it customarily had leaped on his lap where he stroked its purring body. Señora Obregon, a lovely unblemished woman in her forties at the time, left by her deranged husband to fend for her two children and herself after he had been committed to the state mental hospital, had admitted to enjoying the company of cats. She claimed the white cat had always brought her good luck. That such a civilized woman could harbor such a superstition had dumbfounded him, but he had accepted it with the same sympathy she had shown him during his most violent conflicts with his father.

"How are your cats?"

"Oh!" she laughed, and her fine white teeth flashed in the sunlight. "My friends—I had to let go of most of them. But I still have three beautiful angoras, Pila's progeny. They've helped so much. I was very sick." With her long-nailed fingers, she indicated her discoloration. "But I'm all right now. I look different, but that doesn't matter, does it? I have my children. I'm very happy. I'll be joining them in Houston next month."

Américo saw that most of the cars in the cortege had parked along the sidewalk and it was time to carry the casket inside the church.

"You must be going," she said, "I'll leave you alone. It's wonderful to have been able to see you again, though. As I said, it's sad it had to be under these circumstances."

"Thank you, again, for coming."

"Good luck," she said with a knowing smile and kissed him on the cheek.

"Thanks," he said, "I'll need it."

Two men opened the hearse's black doors as Américo took his position ahead of Mavaro. Then, slowly and gently, in tandem with the other pallbearers, Américo helped ease the casket from the hearse and up the steps to the church's entrance. At his back, he heard a car whiz to a stop at the traffic light, where its driver revved the engine. Inside, the car's radio blared a rock 'n' roll song. As they entered the scented shadows of the church, the driver roared down the same street that Johnny had chosen the night he died. The noise sickened Américo.

At the cemetery Américo watched the flag-draped casket roll smoothly from the back of the hearse. The white gloved hands of GI's received it, then carried it beneath the awning where they laid the casket on a wooden stand. Américo, relieved that the GI's had taken over, sat on the front row of metal chairs, with Mavaro next to him, his parents at the other end, and the children in between. His Tio Escolastico sat in the second row, behind Señora Borrego.

The priest came forth and began the ceremony.

"It has been a costly war," he said, his tone marked by authority as he glanced at their faces. "In one form or other, great sacrifices have been required of our young men and their families."

A vast field of simple white crosses on yellow grass arrested Américo's attention. Then he looked up and saw a single buzzard circling high above against the immense sky. It was a splendid Saturday morning, a West Texas morning, bright as silver, on which one could see a hundred miles. His eyes settled on the military installation at the far end of the cemetery.

Not more than three years before, Américo had stood behind the bars of a window on the second floor of the mental ward, delighted. Though not a conscientious objector, he had chosen a drastic means of eluding military service. One night during basic training, pursued by a group of officers and sergeants when he broke rank, he slashed his wrists. A medical discharge proved better than deserting to Canada, too far north and too cold.

In the hospital he had gazed at the patients from the other wards, their limbs in white casts, some of them with parts of their faces destroyed, others in wheelchairs. He felt a mixture of compassion and contempt. It was difficult to wish anyone ill, but these were the same people who in high school, despite his academic accomplishments and promise, had called him a "dumb Mexican" and in basic training had jeered, "Chink!" The bastards respected no one, not even themselves. With his black hair and oriental features, Américo resembled a Viet Cong; that, along with his seething defiance which he invariably voiced, was enough to exclude him from their midst. Others, he knew, had submitted a slew of political arguments for their defiance of the country's wartime policies. His motive was simple—he did not want to squander one more year of his life among the gringos.

So now here he was, back from the brush country of South Texas, where he had found a kind of exile from all this, languishing in the finale of Johnny's misspent youth.

—I volunteered, man.

—You what?

—I volunteered.

—Why? I thought you had joined the Air Force to avoid serving in Vietnam.

—I was bored, man.

Américo disagreed with the priest. The war had not destroyed Johnny. Johnny had been destroyed not by the gringos, but at home by something more evil that had found its way to the heart of the Izquierdo family.

Américo's eyes settled on his father. Señor Izquierdo sat with his arm around Américo's mother, essentially a perfunctory gesture, not something he had ever done genuinely. Américo still had not recovered from the surprise and disbelief that this man of the iron will could look so utterly crushed. Why couldn't he have been this honest with them when Johnny was alive? Did it take the death of his son to show that he too was vulnerable? What now? Would he, in a month or year, sweep all this under the rug and return to his old self—restless, angry, and tyrannical—as if nothing had happened?

—When is Pop coming home? Américo asked. He was a child then.

His mother replied, —Your guess is as good as mine.

—I'm tired of sitting out here night after night on this lawn and waiting for Pop to get home.

—That's the way your father is.

Américo was much older when he said, —I hate Sundays.

—Why?

—Because all you and Pop do is fight.

—Your father is a very hard man. He's crazy. Puerto Rican men are like that. I can't do anything about it. He never listens.

Then came the time that he, Américo, was almost as tall as his father.
—Pop, stop it! Leave her alone!
—That woman has a filthy mouth. I don't want to hear any obscenities in this house.
—Viejo cabron! Go with your putas. Leave us alone! Puto!
—Shut up!
—Pop, don't!
Señor Izquierdo backed away from Señora Izquierdo. —I curse the day, he said, I set foot in this desert. I curse the day I left my country.
In high school it was impossible to study at home.
—Américo!
—What?
—Your father is beating Johnny!
—I know, Mom. I can hear the screams.
—Go in that bedroom and stop him.
—It's none of my business. I'm through with all that bullshit. Nothing I've ever done has stopped anything. If you people want to kill each other, do it. I don't care!
One day Américo and his father sat alone on the porch gazing at the mountains.
—Pop, when is all this going to stop?
—Rico, my children come before anything else in the world. I have worked very hard to give them everything.
Américo detested, with all his soul, the way in which his father dumped Américo and his brothers and sisters in that convenient back-pocket named "my children."
—We have a nice house. My children need a comfortable place, where they can be at peace, where they can play and study. I never had that. I grew up in a bamboo hut the size of this porch. I never had the opportunities my children have. They have food, clothes, money. If they don't take advantage of what I offer them, that's their choice.
—Pop.
—What?
—Will we ever be a happy family? Will all this fighting and yelling ever stop?
—Yes, Rico. One day we are going to be happy, very happy, I promise you. One day we're going to have a house bigger than this one. It'll be a place where all my grandchildren can come and visit me. One day we'll be spending a lot of time together. I know I've been wrong by not spending more time with you. But I'm a hard-working man. Time is money. We wouldn't have all these things if we didn't have money. It's my children's money, and my children come first.

—I'll be leaving soon, Pop.

—But you'll be back. You'll just be gone long enough to get some experience and then, when you have your Ph.D., you'll get a job at the university here. I'll buy you a house, a nice house, where you and your wife can raise my grandchildren. I don't want my grandchildren growing up in a dump. Now that Johnny is back, I have big plans for him too. Johnny will be all right. In fact, I was thinking about one day buying that house across the street so that one of you can live near me. I want all my children to be close to me.

—Pop, Johnny needs help, professional help. He needs to see a psychiatrist.

—All Johnny needs is his father. That's why I'm here, to help him, to do whatever I have to do to get his health back.

—Pop, you've said those things for years. Yet nothing has changed. In fact, things have gotten worse. What's going to happen is that one day you'll find yourself alone in this desert because all your children will have left. Once I leave, I may never come back.

—My children can do whatever they want, but one thing they will never be able to say is that their father never did everything he could for them. You may leave, Rico, but this house will always be your home.

—Izquierdo! called Américo's mother.

Señor Izquierdo glared at her. —What? Can't you see that I'm talking to my son?

—Johnny is turning yellow. He wants to see a doctor.

At the church Américo had fantasized about approaching the old man and saying, as he pointed to the coffin, "This, old man, is what happens when you don't respect your children or your wife. This is what all your lies, your drinking, your women, and your arrogance have done. You deserve every moment of your misery."

The priest made the sign of the cross. Then he removed the cross from the casket and delivered it to Señora Borrego who began crying again. As soon as the priest retired, a GI began playing taps, the longest, saddest taps Américo had ever heard in his life. Everyone began crying; Américo couldn't. The gunfire of the military salute punctuated the weeping.

Américo, after busying himself about the casket as if something had been left unattended, saw his father. The aging man stood alone against a backdrop of white crosses, the American flag under his arm, his shoulders down, his tear-stained face fixed on the coffin. It pained Américo to see him like that. Américo didn't know what to do: to move on or to wait. Then something in him won out. He approached the old man and put his arm around his shoulders, a gesture awkward and frightening because he had seldom done it before. "Come on, Pop. We've got to go home."

Jumping over boulders and cacti, he ran along the *arroyo* with all the energy his young limbs could muster. In his mind he kept seeing the scene he was fleeing: a pool of incandescent water, teeming with glowing fish of all sizes and shapes from whose translucent scales light pulsated. On the surface of the water a dark body floated with its arms dangling loosely from its shoulders, its black hair waving in the water. Red blood oozed from its side and spread gently through the water. Américo stood on the muddy shore, holding a rifle in his hands. As the body rolled over, he saw Johnny's wet face, not yet dead, just unconscious. But Américo knew Johnny was dead. Américo had shot him.

Someone must have already called the police, he thought. They must be speeding in their red-flashing cars towards the levée behind which was the tank filled with water from the mountains. His fear knew no bounds; there was nothing else to do but run and hide in the tunnels where the arroyo emptied.

Inside the tunnel it was dark. His footsteps echoed. He stumbled over stones and tumbleweeds. Now, secure in pitch black darkness, he calmed down and breathed regularly. Coming out the other end of the tunnel, he was surprised to see that things had changed. An orange sunrise pulsated on the distant mountain range. Relieved that no one could say he had been at the levée or prove that he had done anything to his brother, he decided to return home.

At last, after climbing inside his bedroom and lying down, he breathed freely in the knowledge that he had escaped. The only thing that bothered him now was that deep inside he carried a secret no one must ever discover. Even as he dreamed, he knew he was dreaming an old dream, from which he hoped he would never awaken because, awake, he might reveal the secret of what he had done to his brother.

"Américo! Américo!"

He opened his eyes. Sunlight shafted his face.

Dagoberto, his eyes tiny and curious behind his glasses, peered at Américo. "Are you all right? You were talking and moaning in your sleep."

Américo sat up. "I'm okay."

At work that morning, a pile of papers on his desk welcomed him. He sat back in his chair and sipped coffee, glad to be back. The smiles of students and colleagues had filled him with professional self-esteem and purpose. He glanced at the calendar. In another week, Mier, his psychiatrist, would be back from Boston, and things would get back to normal. There was so much Américo wanted to talk to him about. That afternoon he went home feeling much better.

He climbed out of his car, opened the gate, and stepped on the driveway. He looked forward to spending the entire afternoon in his apartment, reading.

A white cat rose from amidst an assortment of toys lying on the grass. A white cat? Cats? He remembered his strange experience with the black one. Where had this one come from? Most of the landlady's cats were grey, tawny, brindled, or calico—an assortment of mongrel cats what wandered into the yard and remained faithfully in the vicinity as long as the landlady fed them and the trash cans were full of edible refuse. It was déjà vu—the white cat crossed his path at almost the same point the black one had.

Señora Obregon's parting words, "Good luck," occurred to him. How silly, he thought as he unlocked the apartment's door. What? Have I cast the responsibility of divining who and where I am upon two innocent felines when the animals of my moods lurk inside me? Don't tell me I'm supposed to sit around now and wait for some good luck? This is absurd.

That evening he dropped in at the Tijuana Jail. Though it had been built on the edge of a deep and wide arroyo, a remote and unlikely spot for a nightclub, it was one of the few good nightclubs in town. In the shadows of the red haze inside, men with cowboy hats stood at the bar while a band, Pobreza, filled the place with the din of cumbias. Américo took a table from where he could see some attractive women with breasts ripe as melons. They were friends of the owners.

The toughest part of coming to Escandon had been leaving Kristina, that lovely, lonely woman from New York. The separation, though absolutely necessary as far as he was concerned and anticipated by both from the beginning of their affair, had been ugly, frightening, and painful. After enjoying for two years the pleasure of cohabitation, he found his now predatory existence distasteful. He needed someone now.

Pura, a sexy Mexican girl, would be nice. But did he want to tangle with her ex-husband, a local cop? The few times Américo had been with her, she had been distractingly frightened that, at any time, her husband might walk through the door and shoot her. What about Marilyn? Hadn't she moved to San Antonio? What was her last name? Marilyn, Marilyn . . . Fitzgibbons—that was it, Marilyn Fitzgibbons. At 10:00 he paid for his drinks and left.

Back at the apartment, its dark rooms resonating with Dagoberto's snores, he turned on the light in the kitchen, called the San Antonio operator, and was given Marilyn's telephone number.

"Hello?" It was a deep throaty voice.

"This is Américo Izquierdo."

"Américo? Are you in town?"

"No, I'm calling you from Escandon."

"What are you doing down there?"

"I live here."

"God, I never imagined you ending up in a hole like that."

"Listen, I was just thinking about you and thought I'd call you up to see if we could get together this weekend."

"Sure. I'd love to see you. Are you still single?"

He grinned, then assured her he was. If he could have, he would have left for San Antonio that moment and climbed into bed with her that night. Instead, after a rambling conversation with his old flame from his student years in El Paso, he went to bed, savoring sweet memories of her legs and breasts.

As he entered Marilyn's apartment, Américo found the situation awkward. When he stormed out of her apartment in El Paso, he had never expected to see her again, having left her for the woman from New York.

Marilyn's smile helped. "I hope you weren't planning on going out to eat tonight," she said, on her way to the kitchen. "I thought I'd cook something."

"I've no plans." He sat down at the nearby table with a bottle of Michelob she'd brought him. "Whatever you want to do is fine with me. It's been a long week. I never thought Friday would get here." He admired the shape of her buttocks and legs in her jeans. "You look very nice. You've lost weight, haven't you?"

She beamed a delighted smile. "Thank you." Michelob in hand, she sat down across. "Well now, tell me everything that's happened to you."

"My brother got killed last week."

She put down her Michelob. "Oh, no!"

He provided her with the essentials of his brother's death, what most people would expect to hear about the loss of a loved one. It would have been too much trouble to tell her more.

She looked off through the smoke untangling from her cigarette. "A tragedy."

When she said nothing more, he asked, "And yourself? How have you been?"

She put down her cigarette and brought another round of beer. "I thought I'd found what I wanted by coming to San Antonio, but I guess I didn't. This year has been hell."

She explained. Not more than a month before, she had for the last time broken off a relationship with a black man. "I still haven't accepted it. It's very depressing."

"What happened to what's-his-name?"

"Arguindegui?" She rolled eyes. "That poor ball-less jerk. I think he's married, married a Mexican girl, probably has ten children by now. He never finished school. He's back living in a barrio in El Paso."

She complained that San Antonio suffered from a dearth of the sort of man that interested her, by which Américo understood her to mean eligible young professionals on their way up. Somehow he found that difficult to believe.

"According to a friend of mine," she said, "the only thing that matters to the under-thirty male is what crosses in front of his dick."

Américo grinned. It seemed ironic for Marilyn to say that; after all, she had once told him, with a substantial amount of braggadocio, that she had bedded more than a hundred men before turning twenty-five. But she did seem lonely. In the end, loneliness got everyone. He stood up.

He ran his fingers through her hair. She was young and attractive in a plain-faced sort of way, with an ever-watering pretty red mouth, which, taking her cheeks between his hands, he kissed lavishly.

When he stopped, she whispered in his ear. "I was wondering how long you were going to take to do that."

"I don't like to be rushed."

She got up. "The food won't be ready for another hour. Why don't you take a shower, get into something more comfortable?"

After supper, Marilyn disappeared into the bathroom while Américo wandered into her bedroom to wait for her. He put his bottle of Michelob on the nightstand, then stepped out of his robe and crawled between the pink satin sheets of a queen-sized bed and propped himself up on a fat shiny pillow. Listening to the hum of the shower in the bathroom, he closed his eyes. The tension in his limbs had been evaporated by a hot shower. The food had been excellent. And now, as he lay in this cozy bedroom, his naked limbs graced by satin sheets, he marvelled at his good fortune. Tonight he would sleep until every cell in his body was satisfied. There was nothing like a woman to get you back to your senses.

The noise of the shower ceased. Marilyn walked into the room with a towel wrapped about her head and her figure clad in black terrycloth. Américo finished off his beer and moved to the end of the bed, where he lay half-wrapped in a satin sheet, his head propped up by his hand as he watched her sit before her vanity mirror.

With her blue eyes fixed on her face in the softly lit mirror, she began blow-drying her chestnut hair. It puffed up. Soon the horrible electronic noise stopped, and she brushed her hair into shape. Next came the application of makeup from which emerged a new woman with sparkling lips and sensual eyes.

She glanced at him through the mirror. "Your voice has changed."

That surprised him. "Have I acquired an accent?"

"No. Just a different timbre of voice, kind of singsongy."

"I've been speaking a lot of Spanish."

"How do you like Escandon?"

"Cultural shock."

"Is it different from El Paso?"

"It's another country. A lost society, someone said. But that's why I went there, to de-Anglicize myself."

She laughed. "Oh, Américo, are you still into all that identity bit?"

"My Spanish has improved by leaps and bounds."

"I never knew you had a problem speaking Spanish."

"I did."

"The next thing I'll hear about you is that you got married to some pretty Mexican señorita."

Américo grinned. "Right now all I want to do is get my three years of teaching experience, which is what I need to get a job outside the country. As soon as I get that, I'm leaving."

"Are you serious?"

"Dead serious. The only reason I settled for the job in Escandon was that I couldn't find one outside the country."

"Where do you want to go? Mexico?"

"Anywhere. As long as it's not the United States."

She turned and looked at him. "You're just going through a bad time. I don't believe you'll ever leave."

She put away her cosmetics, then looked at herself in the mirror in that womanly, self-absorbed way that had always delighted and perplexed Américo about women and their beauty. Quite nonchalantly, she slipped out of her terrycloth which she let fall about her buttocks, and sat there in a casual, frank display of her naked body. As she dashed perfume on herself, Américo's eyes consumed the length of her sturdy back, her shoulders and the way her hair fell on them, and her pink-nippled breasts in the vanity mirror. She rose with a smile and climbed in bed with him.

Hours later, Américo found himself lying on the bed, face down, exhausted. When he peeped back at Marilyn, she lay next to him, her back propped up on a rich pillow, one leg crossed over another as she smoked a cigarette.

With her other hand, she stroked his back. "I don't know what that woman from New York did for you, but whatever it was, she did a good job. You've changed a lot."

Américo closed his eyes.

Yuccas stood on both sides of a desolate mountain path. After a long hard climb, Américo, so tired he didn't think he could go much farther, decided to rest where the path curved. A plume of white smoke, seeping from among the rocks, surprised him as it slowly materialized into the shape of a man.

It was Johnny.

—Is this a dream? Américo asked himself. Yes, that's what it is. It's a dream.

But it wasn't a dream either, as he found out when he touched Johnny.

—You're alive! shouted Américo. You really are alive!

In his customary hangdog manner, Johnny said, —Man, was that a long sleep!

Américo, unable to contain his enthusiasm, wanted to get back and tell everyone that it had all been a mistake.

—Look, Johnny, he said, we need to get back. Mom and Pop will be ecstatic when they see you. Do you think you can handle the long climb down the mountain?

—You know me, Rico. Climbing down the side of this dinosaur ain't no big deal.

—In fact, said Américo, things will be better now, better than when all those horrible things began happening to us.

Johnny, instead of accompanying Américo down the mountain, took off in the opposite direction. Américo felt the old anger he always felt when Johnny insisted on having his own way, especially when he was so obviously wrong.

—No, not that way, said Américo. That's not the way down the mountain.

—Yeah, it is, Rico. Come on!

—No, not that way, Johnny! cried Américo. Come back!

But Johnny, stubborn as ever, trudged on up the mountain path and disappeared beyond the curve.

—This is not a dream. Johnny isn't dead. I must find him.

Américo ran.

—Johnny! he screamed with all his might.

"What's the matter?"

It was dark. He sat up. He saw Marilyn. "Oh, it's you."

"You screamed."

"What time is it?"

"It's about four."

Américo understood. "Go back to bed. I'll be all right."

In the kitchen he found a Coke and Marilyn's cigarettes. In the living room he opened a window and sat down on the highbacked chair, feeling the cool air touch his bare legs. He released a billow of smoke.

With everything seemingly so far away, removed by the night of the Texas expanse, he felt an immense loneliness and sadness descend upon him. It was an old ache from a wound not yet healed.

The station wagon came to a stop at the traffic light. Johnny sat in the back seat. Américo and his father had been fighting from the time they left the house. The night before he had seen his father dragging his mother by her hair across the living room floor. Américo had not wanted to intervene, as he had on so many other occasions, but he did so when he saw his mother spit blood.

Américo jumped from the car. —I don't respect you as a man or a father! I detest you!

As he hurried along the sidewalk, he heard a car bounce over the curb. He turned and saw his father's enraged face behind the car's steering wheel. If Américo had not run up the steps and been shielded by a stone wall, his father would have hit him. The car crashed against the stone wall.

Américo glared at his father, who backed away and hot-rodded down the boulevard. —You fucking Puerto Rican asshole!

Américo spent the entire day at Señora Obregon's house.

—I don't want to go back to that house, he said to Señora Obregon.

—I wish I could stay here. I hate them—peasants, barbarians. They're such stupid people. Do you know what my mother told me when I asked her once if I could learn to play the violin? She said, 'No. It sounds like a cat.'

Señora Obregon laughed. —That's not her fault, Américo. Your background is different from hers.

—I feel like an utter stranger in that house. I'm willing to accept the

fact that they're peasants, but I refuse to accept the need for all that violence. God, how I wish I could leave!
—It's very late.
—Thank you for everything.

It was a long walk in the night, about fourteen city blocks, but he took it slowly because he wanted to arrive at twelve o'clock. Maybe his father would be asleep by then. But his father was waiting for him and stopped Américo on the way to his bedroom.

—The school principal called me at work. Why didn't you go to school?

Américo stared at the short, handsome man whose sturdy body seemed to have been built to cut sugarcane all day. —I didn't go to school because I didn't want to go. So fucking what?

—No son of mine talks to me like that.

The lights came on. Américo's mother, brothers, and sisters emerged from their bedrooms.

—I told you last night to keep your hands off Mom. When you earn my respect, I'll treat you with respect.

—I pay the bills in this house!

—I don't give a shit what you pay!

—Don't talk to your father like that!

Américo knew his father might strike him at any moment, but he didn't care any more. He was ready for anything.

—I'll talk to you any way I want, old man.

His father shouted, —Leave this house at once!

Américo, outraged to the point of intoxication, ran to his bedroom where he took from his closet a small black .22 pistol a friend of his had lent him. There was no other way out—he was going to settle this problem once and for all.

As he went to look for his father, who was now screaming at Américo's mother in the kitchen, Mavaro and Johnny jumped him. The gun went off. Screams filled the room. Mavaro wrested the pistol from his hand. Américo, sitting up, looked to see who had been shot, but no one had been hurt. The bullet had shattered the large gold-framed mirror in the living room.

Holed up that night in his bedroom, Américo gazed out the window facing the eastern horizon, barely visible at night, and swore that one day, as soon as he was able, he would leave and never come back. If he could not kill his father with a pistol, he would kill him in another way.

As he looked out the window of the woman's apartment where he was staying, he wondered why things had turned out that way. Was there nothing he could have done to change things?

Back in elementary school when his brother, scared and crying, had come to look for Américo, Américo was disgusted. Now he forgot what the problem had been, but he clearly remembered that, after talking to Johnny's teacher and clearing up the problem, he had looked at his brother and seen how hopelessly lost the pretty boy looked. His foreboding was confirmed in high school by Johnny's slashing and stealing of tires, followed by his slashing of a boy's arm with a stiletto.

"Join the army and become a man," Américo had taunted his brother. Now it seemed to have been a stupid thing to have told him.

Yes, Américo had left his hometown with the expectation of never returning and leaving his past behind, but it had not worked out like that. His rage sparkled in the darkness of his unconscious like the horns of a bull desirous of blood. Nor had his old longing subsided. There were moments when, if he could have killed his father and gotten away with it, he would have. So far, even with help from his psychiatrist, there seemed to be no relief in sight for him. Though he had murdered no one, he felt like a criminal condemned to wander the earth, alone and self-absorbed, without hope of redemption.

The orange streaks of an incipient sun touched the brocaded curtain. Slowly, the birth of the new day revealed the city. He got up. In the bedroom Marilyn lay sound asleep. Her white buttocks turned golden in the growing light. As he climbed in bed with her, she sensed him and rolled over, resting her arm across his chest and a breast against his arm. At times she had disgusted him with her promiscuity and vulgarity, but at that moment her golden nakedness was a fragrant ointment which salved, if only for the moment, the broken part of him.

Américo wandered off aimlessly a short distance from the gasoline pump where Dagoberto had parked his new sedan. He inhaled the storm-cleansed air as he watched a long string of headlights floating slowly along the glossy wet street. Some children in plastic raincoats pushed and tilted against each other as they walked by. Two girls stopped at the curb. Fascinated by the current swelling at their feet, they stood silently until one of them slipped off her shoes and waded into the water, yelling at the others to join her. Américo found it refreshing to see the children in the water, risking the splashing of cars, unthreatened.

Was it the rain? The physical exhaustion after the long drive home from San Antonio that morning? A fine mood soon to be pre-empted by a foul one? He felt different, cleansed, at the center of himself. Was it possible to feel like this all the time? Not merely once in a while? To live daily poised at the center of a rushing maelstrom of absurdities without being rent asunder?

Several young men sat on the porch of a wooden shack across the street. One of them, beer bottle in hand, was slouched against the side of the house, a red bandanna tied about his head. He looked up and casually returned Américo's gaze. The face struck him—it could have been Johnny's.

He turned away and walked towards the car. Ya, Johnny, he thought, Let me be! He climbed in the sedan with Dagoberto, and they left.

The dreary wooden houses and muddy dirt streets of Escandon assaulted Américo. Many people had told him it was the ugliest city they had ever seen in their lives. He liked the palm trees; they reminded him of Puerto Rico, where his father had been born and raised. But if his father visited him, he would have berated him for having moved to such a hellhole, the last place his father would want to see his grandchildren raised.

"Did you have a good time in San Antonio?"

Américo shifted in his seat. "My friend was very nice. But driving back today was rough. I didn't think I was going to make it back. It rained so hard I couldn't see a thing ahead of me. I wanted to stop, park by the side of road. But it let up by the time I got to Cotulla."

They fell silent. After a while, Dagoberto said to Américo, "I know you've been in a lot of pain. I just wanted to let you know that I've been praying for you."

Américo, unconvinced prayer had ever done anybody much good, nodded in acknowledgment.

"Was your brother a spiritual person?"

Américo glanced at Dagoberto. What the hell did that have to do with his brother's death? Then Américo remembered that Dagoberto and he were very different. "No."

"What was your brother like?"

"Crazy . . . like me."

"You're not crazy."

Dagoberto slowed down and turned into a side street, where he parked on high ground. Américo climbed out of the car and beheld the same mess he had seen when he arrived from San Antonio that morning—a dirt street gutted by rain and flooded by pools of muddy water. There was only one way to cross the street to their apartment: on a wooden plank between two pools of water, which Dagoberto negotiated easily. No big deal, thought Américo, as he stepped forward.

Américo felt the plank tilt underfoot—"Oh, shit!"—before he slipped off it and hit the water flat on his face. It was deeper than he had expected, and cold. For a moment he was so disgusted he didn't want to get up—just wanted to lie there and, if he could, drown. Instead, his hands and knees found solid ground. He rose. After spitting grit and wiping his eyes, he beheld Dagoberto who gaped at him from the sidewalk. Américo blinked and looked again. A brindled cat, which had appeared from God knows where, sat by Dagoberto's foot in absolute stillness. Américo didn't know whether to cry or burst into a fit of laughter.

ease

SYLVIA GIRON

    prefer disgust
    they do they do and that
    is why they build
    giant gems
    lustfully in agreement
    they go home and
    rape their wives
    to the music
    of the ten o'clock news
        this is what
        kind of nation?

        still
    they expect to see
    their own ghosts and
    sometimes they do

Science

HENRY RAEL JR.

Small pieces of paper fall slower
than large ones, no matter what
Galilleo says
The same gravity which holds cities
to the brown,
>gentle earth saturates
>me like oil in a sponge
>wrapping itself around
>my every cell
pulling down

Newton's theory of gravitation says
that the gravitational force between two
objects is proportional to the size of their
masses
>Although my body is larger than yours,
>your mass must be several thousand times
>that of mine, as your attraction to me is
>so painfully minimal
>>while it is all I can do to
>>sacrifice only my eyes to
>>your esoteric magnetism

My hands have never caressed the magnificence
of your inviting skin and even my eyes are
>cautious as they sweep across you
>>like a moist tongue on dripping ices
>(you don't have to take off your clothes for
>me, just *say* that you will)

Something is very wrong with physics,
because I cannot attract even your
   lightest glance while to you my
entire self will happily fall
      like a lead feather.

I can't place the problem
   but I am dazzled by the wonders
   of your science, alarmed by your
   seduction as you sit
   oblivious to my
   hapless struggle with gravity.

Evolution by Night

ERYC BOURLAND

She made my changes at night
and when she was done, I swore
my simple love for a Salem witch. On
small hairy feet
I walked upright for her.
And she held me in leaves,
ran through my evolution with me
and touched my dented forehead
and fed me bits of hairy cheese.

She spat at the pile of seasoned wood,
which wouldn't smoke and smother her
but burn cool, and slowly cook her.
She touched me one time
and was cindered at the stake,
clutching coarse hairs from my back.
And I rolled in her ashes, racking,
finding charred witch skin
still pale,
and dried witch hair
still soft—
what they burned was simian and simple.

By night she shaped me
into something closer to her.
Broke me to her.
Lying in her ashes
I rubbed her into my skin
and I tasted stale cheese,
and I smelled her palms
like they once were
when she held them to my head.
No one knows how the monkey feels.

Why it is better to read some afternoons

JUDI LYNNE JUDY

She would agree to wait for him, the idiotic walls painted lime and pink. There would be a motion of stillness. Answers

themselves coming up for breath, the horse and its cream telephone, the telephone horse.

Such a definition, marigolds torn in a stingy little hand. Lilacs and their bizarre alcovian scents.

Why would the sky twist itself into the image of a man in braids, or the image of a gypsy? Why would it be Saturday?

The scene is Boston, and somewhere in the drip desert of New Mexico. Old women dance around a fire waving sticks.

We do not know what sort of sticks. Perhaps juniper or aspen. Motivation or a theory of waiting, could have been what prompted

her to lay down. Stripping back her pants a second thought of somewhat startling proportion. Her and a rocket ship.

Flying in pairs, doves weave the sentences in twos. Tiny pieces of shattered light held fast to their tongues.

This is all an accelerated dream she said. The planet dissolves simultaneously as someone stirs Alka-Seltzer. The next life written in threes.

Dream Fragment Thirty

ROY RICCI

I remember once staring upon
   The twilight of All Soul's Day
     while white shrouds of broken clouds
descended upon Van Cortlandt Park Lake.

I transform the greenery of white oak
   and deep purple maples, to stately saguaro
   cactus alongside calcified arroyos,
   where white faced heifers are always
this close
     to thirst, death, and ravens.

I stop atop the pine coned ridgeline
   of the sloping Manzano Mountains.
   Dismount my broken shoed palomino
   and remove from my weather worn saddle bag
   Six Calimyrna figs
   and one by one
            skip them
   like brown unknown stones
   over the cliff   sight unseen.

L. V. QUINTANA

I wonder what happened, whatever happened
to that girl, Judy, Judy was her name
who would follow me, would follow me after school
determined, so determined for a kiss, just a kiss
She was coy, pretended to be so coy and was
perhaps, perhaps a little
I supposed I teased her, yes, I teased her
Truth is I wanted her, wanted her just as much
as much
Oh I could have, oh so easily, so easily
My hands over or even under the blouse
of her Catholic school uniform touched
her breasts, small but not too for a seventh grader
Jesus, Jesus, Jesus, Judy, Judy, Judy
So long ago, a place called home I think about
now and then, often, today and today also about Judy
and how she was one of the few who ever loved me there

L. V. QUINTANA

Cardinal Mindszenty
Perhaps I should say a prayer for you today
Dead at eighty three
The nuns praised you every morning of the eighth grade
when the communists were throwing people into meatgrinders
and the only record I had enough nerve to dance to was
Blueberry Hill
In complete and total exile from your beloved Hungary
I remember Ginger's body in a tight skirt;
just looking could cause you to commit a hundred sins
Hero of a war we never understood
I never learned to jitterbug
Every morning we prayed for peace in the world
One morning before Mass José told me his grandmother
had cursed the governor and his commodities
in her dying breath
I wore a black leather jacket
Perhaps I should have said a prayer for you today
One O'clock. Two O'clock. Three O'clock Rock

Santorini

JAMES RUPPERT

I've known this white before.
The island soaks a drying sun
like Las Cruces or Juarez. Crust
of sediment on alkali flats,

but here cities peak over
lava face, hundreds of feet,
edging the caldera, staring
into its own wake. A small cone

centers the jutting cliffs.
Falling to the outer sea, a
gentle slope revives what death
covered in ash, shook in terror

the ancient volcano blew myth high
as pieces of civilization and
Atlantis sunk in on itself—
all overladen worlds do.

The desert shines a sparse white
to hide the fossil sea beneath.
Unique, the taste of island wine
no hint of ash disturbs.

Balanced, tourist and town on a precipice
All stare where sea and sky blend.
Above us, the radar station sits
heavy on the mountain top waiting

for Turkish jets. Silent, a
Byzantine monastery shares its view.
Both hoard their relics, live in
order. Assorted bones of saints and

pictures of tearful, bleeding Christs.
When a monk dies, silently they
shelf his gleaming, skull white,
the ossarium candle-lit

eyes holes wide, mesmerized
fixed on the heart of the cone
the certain date of death
painted on his forehead.

For My Daughter

BAYITA GAROFFOLO

I want to stay
put my nose in the smell of your neck
open the skin that burns your infant eyes
closed, but I'm in the hollow of cold.
My breath blows brittle at the door.

The weight of your stare as you crawl
and reach for my breast, pulls
skirting each rib.
I am lost in its grip, crazed
and icebound to the room.

Impatient now, your bird-eyes split
an overflow of wet drools
like rain over wet sand,
and slips staccato on your warm tongue.
Your arm, wing-light, drags it away.

A calm thaw slides over my face.
The startled gaze that froze
the pleas in your throat when I began
to leave, is gone. Your sighs slow down
I can move my toes,

go after all from here to where
wild plum grows loose-jointed
under the piñon jay, and come back
to hold you over and over
on the slopes of my thighs,
and whisper hello.

Monastery of Christ in the Desert
Abiquiu, New Mexico
Antiphon

BAYITA GAROFFOLO

Sing before eating
bread with syrup from the apricot tree.
Don't talk about weather
or what you'll do all day.
Walk in whispers back to your room
and write about the cochineal plant
you saw on the road. Lie on the floor
stretch lean from the eyes down
pray that your leg-lifts
clear the kerosene lamp by the bed.
Run a mile away from the bells at Terce
down two hills to the no-hunting sign
and back. Sit in a leather chair
in an empty room
by the river on a rock.
Step fast under water too hot
for the average soul.
Hold coarse words in their place
as you drip on the floor.
Heat the kettle for tea
write, remembering you're a guest
remembering the order of things.

Colors in the Valley

JAMES MACKIE

The long ridge curves precisely, rising
almost to a bowl where the sun is on the horizon.
Is there a miracle in the drop of water
slithering down the brown stalk?
The curling worm circles,
bone is not the logic.
A shabby tree burns in this light.
A crow black and silver black
flips in out of the leveled sun.
Here whales knew the unroundness of blue,
the pressed texture of green.
The west is an orange rim, the rock red.
The light recedes to an infinite gray.

Points of Departure

JEFFREY N. JOHNS

At times, a dim speck of light appears in the mirror—a headlight in the receding distance. It rises and falls, floating in the cold, damp air. When it is most indistinct, it seems to have its greatest effect, reflecting a hot pinpoint of light onto my chest and scalding the soft tissues of the heart below. I rub hard across the rib cage as if to pulverize and disperse the pain. But the stinging hurt just buries itself deeper. I skid the motorcycle to a stop and turn to look, but—like an ill-defined star that shines when viewed obliquely, then disappears under direct scrutiny—the light is gone. There is only the lonely tundra, the slate-cold grey sky, and the unseen presence that bends the willows. I rev the engine, engage the gears, and press the black skin of tires into the mud and gravel that vaguely suggest a road. Soon, the whistling of air in my drafty helmet rises to a high pitch, and I float headlong through the nearly forgotten terrain.

The huge, strange land seems to swallow the rattling of my engine; I glance down at the reflection in the shiny fuel tank to make sure it hasn't swallowed me as well. The tundra stretches out for a distance I cannot gauge, to an elusive range of blue-white mountains whose peaks are obscured by icy mist. A raven swoops across my path like a sentinel from the surrounding wilderness. Then it turns and glides back to its hidden outpost. I feel separate from it and its universe, as if I am an alien on the surface of a distant world. In a way, I feel superior to this outland of disordered mountains and unreasoning animals, yet it is odd that I should be so in awe of it, while it is so unconcerned with me.

As the wind plays its eerie tune, I recall last night's dream. There was a fire outside my tent. Like some Viking or Gothic barbarian, he sat in its glow, stoking the tinder with something long and white. His ruddy skin shimmered in the blaze, and his golden hair floated above like a savage nimbus. He faced the fire, but—as always—his watery eyes focused on something else, something distant in time and space. "You're the only one that knows about these," he said without turning away from the blaze. His large frame seemed even bigger than in life, and his powerful hands stronger, more dangerous. I sensed something odd about the fire, but it took all my energy to tear my mesmerized gaze away from him and focus on the flames. It was not wood that fueled the leaping tongues of fire, but bones. He gripped a thigh bone near the hip and pushed others toward a skull which rested in the center, flames curling around its eye sockets and gaping jaws. I opened my mouth to scream, but—as if my larynx had been ripped out—only a pitiful fluttering of air came forth. "Now that you're leaving, I have to make sure no one else will find out about them," he said. Then he rose and walked off into the blackness.

"We're all killers," he had once said. "The civilized hide from the bloodletting. But the blood flows anyway, in hidden streams that run through our unconscious." Perhaps he felt the hot currents of my own unseen rivers, and trusted me as a brother with the knowledge of his crime. Perhaps he considered me too strong to reveal his secret—or too weak to face his madness if I did.

At the far shore of this vast plateau of soggy muskeg and stunted spruce trees, the land drops off toward the sea. Across the water I will feel safe again, and free. But the miles pass slowly through the mud and sporadic rain, across this amphitheater of nature on whose stage I feel so meaningless and unwanted.

A small bridge lies ahead. I press the wet leather toe of my boot down on the brake pedal and bring the bike to a stop along the embankment. In the distance, two gravel-choked streams merge to form the river which passes below. I want to hear the flowing waters, but the hissing and sputtering engine crowds them out. I kill the engine and take off my helmet. The cool air and silence of the tundra converge on my damp, naked face and head. I walk across the spongy ground toward the little river. Its gurgling rises from the bank. It is soothing. I almost lose myself in its gentle melody: I nearly relax. But something makes me turn back, to the muddy road that snakes off behind. The road is empty. But still, it makes me think of him, and whether he is following. The burning pain inside my rib cage starts up again, and I rub my fist across the spot to make it go away. I rub enough pain into the muscle to obscure the sting below. But I have also smothered the grey waters into silence. A breath of chill air swirls about my ears, rumbling like distant thunder. I hurry back across the sweating muskeg skin and feel in the saddlebag for the revolver, buried there beneath layers of clothing. The engine grinds hesitantly, then catches and sputters in the lifeless air.

It is twilight now, as dark as it will get this far north in the heart of summer. The buzzing of hungry mosquitoes is fading away outside the tent. Are they becoming drowsy? Or just saving their energy for a chance at my pungent, unwashed flesh tomorrow morning? The brandy tastes good and relaxes me. I wonder which of my traveler's dreams will come tonight: the old one in which I stay in a tall wooden house overlooking a highway with no traffic, where the land beyond is not real but only a roadmap, leading nowhere; or the new one, with the fire and the bones. A timber wolf howls. I imagine him poised on a distant promontory, surveying the tableland below for something weak and slow, on whose flesh he may continue his survival. I pull the sleeping bag tight around my neck, having little doubt which dream will fill the half-darkness of my night.

The honking of Canada geese and rattling call of a kingfisher wake me at four a.m. The sun has already begun its boomerang loop around the grey-blue sky. The mosquitoes are waiting for me on the netting of the tent. Their frantic buzzing rises with the warming sun. But there is another sound resonating in the distance. Its volume swells until it drowns out the droning of the mosquitoes. Then its pitch descends. There is a crunching of gravel. I bolt forward and peer through the fragile netting. The motorcycle and its rider flash into view then disappear toward the lake a short distance away. As I reach beneath the leather jacket for the gun I have never used, my hand is shaking and feels weak as a child's.

The pounding of the engine ceases suddenly. I wait for a long while, hoping he will leave, but there is only stillness. I dress quietly then slowly unzip the tent door. He is sitting on the lake bank, looking out toward the smooth water. Surely he has seen my camp—there is no choice but to confront him.

As I approach, a small flock of loons floats carelessly on the lake near where he sits, but as I move closer, they paddle away toward the far shore, their whistle-like calls skimming over the water like flat stones. Though he must be aware of my presence, he does not acknowledge it. His eyes are watery and squinting, focusing on something remote. I fight to keep my fear pure and sharp, but it begins to muddy itself with guilt and pity.

"I didn't think you would come," I say, each word falling from my lips like pregnant lies. As if the words have difficulty settling in his mind, his response comes slowly.

"I just wanted to travel with you for a while longer," he says pitifully. He is like a wolf wounded in a fight, whining through blood-drenched fangs, but sure to strike at whoever comes too near.

"Look, I have to get out of here and make a fresh start," I say.

"What you mean is, you don't feel comfortable around killers anymore." There is insolence in his voice now. He unsheathes the hunting knife that hangs from his belt and begins to pare the young bark from a willow twig, exposing the moist, yellow-green sapwood core. With each stroke, his jacket rises above the small of his back, revealing the black metal barrel of an automatic pistol. "You think the people on the other side are innocent," he says, "just because their hands are clean and white. But let me tell you something. They're the worst ones. They've denied being killers for so long, that now they believe in their innocence. Their slaughter is blind and irreverent: it will consume them one day, and it will swallow you as well, if you join them."

He drives the bleaming knife blade into the soft earth of the lake bank and looks at me for the first time. His eyes are confused. There is a wild madness there, capable of vanquishing all reason.

My mouth is trembling. "I'm sorry," I say. "I don't understand. I just know that I can't live like this anymore." Unsteadily, I turn and walk away, listening closely for any movement and watching the ground for his shadow next to mine.

As I pack my gear, I keep my eyes on him: he is unmoving. I straddle the seat of the motorcycle. On the lake beyond where he sits, the loons are returning, gliding over the sleek waters. A cold, disengaged emptiness hangs in the morning air. I start the engine and pull away. Before I round the bend past the lake, a single gunshot cracks the silence, echoes, then fades away across the tundra. I do not look back, not even into the mirror.

Leonor Dreams of Sor Juana

ALICIA GASPAR DE ALBA

if I could rub myself
along your calf,
feel your knee
break the waters of my shame;

if I could lay my cheek
against the tender sinews
of your thigh,
smell the damp
cotton that Athena
never wore, her blood
tracks steaming in the snow;

if I could forget
the devil and the priest
who guards my eyes
with pitchfork and with host;

if I could taste
the bread, the blood, the salt
between your legs
as I taste mine;

if I could turn myself
into a bee and free
this soul, those bars
webbed across your window
would be vain, that black
cloth, that rosary, that crucifix—
nothing could save you
from my sting.

Caldo de Pollo

ALICIA GASPAR DE ALBA

Recipe:

This evening the rain calls
for chicken soup,
thighs boiling their yellow skins
into a broth spiced
with rosemary, basil, and rue—
thoughts of death as thick
as the garlic cloves and the carrots,
more transparent than the onions.

Memory:

A week before my thirtieth birthday
I remember a prediction made by a drunken woman
who fancied herself psychic.

Photograph:

I sit in my one-year-old skin
in the center of a ring of relatives,
my fat fingers hooked
around the neck of a beer bottle.

Three of the six other people in the picture
died in a space of fifteen years:
Grandpa and two uncles.

Prediction:

At thirty, said the drunken woman,
you will join the semi-circle of the dead.

Truth:

The girl died
and became the drunken woman.
The beer bottles and the hard-boiled bones
are in the trash.
The carrots and the grandfather stopped breathing.
The drunken woman climbed the wagon
of dreams and went North.
And the broth boils on,
the chicken blood spiced with rosemary,
the sweet basil of possibility,
the rue and the onions and the garlic
becoming
caldo de pollo,
tonic for a rainy night.

29 skins ago, I did not know the recipe.

Picking up the License

J. DIANNE DUFF

For obscure reasons the police kept
his driver's license after the death
Monday I was instructed by postcard
to claim it in rm. 305
in the evidence section
so I wear stockings   heels
pretty green skirt to insure
an efficient state of mind
I am a pro at the business side
of death by now
several detectives tease
ladies behind the counter
one man I knew in high school
and didn't think much about
but now he is so bearlike
friendly in regular clothes
I am grateful to compare
number and ages of our children
I like this
place where tragedy and murder
happen and people joke around
so functionally ugly
the woman who took my card
laughed a high child's laugh
at the detectives' jokes
returns now from a back room
with hinges but no door
she is good   her hair
is brown   her eyes lift
so good at this she looks
deep into my face   then away
kindly spills out "evidence"

for me to "examine"
motorcycle registration
a driver's license   I had never
seen his driver's license
certainly nothing he would show
girlfriends or even a sister
that funny unflattering smile
I had forgotten for a time
he curled his mustache
the unkind bureau light caught
a reflection in an upper corner
creating the illusion of a shroud
over the face that looked like mine
over the familiar silly smile
this is the end of any business
I can do today.

Oscar Comes Through New Mexico from El Salvador

MAISHA BATON

That night, in a fastfood restaurant
just off the University district,
it occurred to me
the time to speak of El Salvador had come;
to speak of Oscar passing through New Mexico;
death threats barking at his heels;
the dread of another summer chasing him
through long alleys of America;
through bloodied streets already rotting
with the dreams of migrant farmers;
mothers carrying their babies
secretly in their bellies;
papas always looking for *trabajo*.
Oscar with his long fingers and dark eyes.

All night we held each to the other
as if we could bridge the distance
of language.
"*Voy al norte! Voy al norte!*" he whispered.
His awful sadness pierced my bold armor.
His losses were my losses.
(I am only an ethnic after all; a war baby
100 years after emancipation
still seeking freedom; still seeking *trabajo*.

Oh Oscar, El Salvador is no more your land
than mine.
The unmarked grave of your mother
is now our mutual burden.
Your flight, no different than
the flight of my fathers.
"El norte! El norte!" they cried
and (like yourself) disappeared
into the background of America.

dare to un-do
masks

MARK FUNK

        him got bad scars
              big messy victory scars
      brown eyes like teddy bear
             marine/vietnam stuff/icky
                 hard to look at
for a minute feel panic this hitchhiker
        his face resewn sloppy roads red tissue
nose not quite healed, threatening
      could have used more stitches
wanted off at indian school road
        "going to a church party for the elderly"
              (he must have been a scream)
      "must be five-ish," i say "don't wear a watch"
he say you ever been in the armed forces
     naahh   (me)
     humm   (he)
             "here's just fine. stop here"
he shake short stubby strong grip
            "thank you, sir."
      wades across intersection still alive to
parking lot church of christ rearview mirror i
      see him read large note on front doors
drive forward ten shocks
        next time glance mirror image—no marine
            no lie   true story
i am face-to-face with my front door
      wrong key   he was real

The Visitor

LAYLE SILBERT

Some people knew whether they were supposed to use the front door or the back door. During the day mostly it was the back door, which was why Mama kept the back door locked. But you could always see who it was on the back porch wanting to get in by looking through the glass pane in the top of the back door or the window next to it giving out on the back stairs. Usually a peddler was selling soap or raffle tickets, once in a while the ice man. "Ice today, missus?" he'd say, his tongs over his shoulder from having just delivered ice to the people upstairs. Sometimes Mama waited at the railing and hollered out to a fruit peddler, "Yoohoo! A pound of apples and a peck of potatoes." Pretty soon a raggedy man came running up the stairs because he didn't want to leave his horse without him.

This time it was different. The door was locked, the day was sunny and huge patches of sunshine came through the door pane and the window into the kitchen, warm and smelling of fresh food. A large pale chicken lay in a pot, and vegetables waited on the cutting board for the right moment to go into the pot, too. Mama was kneading dough complaining her hands hurt. Ellen waited for her chance to lick the remains of the makings of the cake for supper tonight.

They heard a knock, the most timid, lightest knock in the world. Who was it? Mama looked up all alert. Again a light knock. Would she let the knocker go away? She went to the window to look. "It's a little man," she said. "He couldn't hurt anybody."

From where Ellen sat she couldn't see a hair of the visitor, if that's what he was going to be. She was supposed to be doing homework, but always had time for something new.

Mama unlocked the door and there he was, a small, thin man with a wispy, black beard, a black hat like a rabbi's and a shabby suit. A toe in a sock with a hole in it stuck out of one shoe. The other shoe was all right except that he needed new shoelaces.

"Yes," said Mama, not at all afraid.

He looked frail and harmless.

Speak, she seemed to command. Finally she said, "Whatever you're selling, we don't need it."

The man looked as if he'd just stopped crying. Did he need a handkerchief? Never had Ellen heard of somebody begging for a handkerchief. He didn't want one at all, because he said, "I'm hungry, missus," and rubbed his stomach or rather where his stomach should be. He looked to have no stomach at all.

"Hungry?" Mama echoed. "That's all? Wait a minute." She closed the door leaving him standing outside, wiped her hands, opened the bread box and cut an exceptionally thick slice of pumpernickel, put it on a paper napkin and opened the door. "Here, eat," she said.

He looked at the bread and said, "You have some butter maybe?" looking surprised at himself for asking.

"Butter?" Mama sighed and said. "All right, I'll get you butter. You might as well come in and sit down." How could this little man hurt anybody?

He made a small formal bow like an actor and entered the kitchen with the air of somebody who might soon rub his hands with pleasure.

"Sit down." Mama pulled up a chair.

He sat down.

Now Mama was going to wait on him. Ellen knew what Mama thought of waiting on people. She was against it. Everybody should wait on himself. That was how these matters were conducted in their house. Mama set the bread down and the butter dish next to it along with a butter knife.

"Eat," she said again.

Ellen moved around to see better, watched the new person from across the table. The visitor broke off a piece of bread, buttered it as thickly as the bread would hold and stuffed it into his mouth. Again he looked as if he were crying. But there were no tears. "M'm," he said, broke off another piece, ate it, took another, then ate it too.

Mama cut another piece, thicker than the others and handed him more butter. He'd used up a whole stick.

Mama wasn't complaining. Instead she watched, her hands on the back of a chair, its seat shoved under the table. Wasn't that how people watch a snake, careful not to get too close while not wanting to move away so as not to miss anything? "You're hungry yet?" she smiled as she spoke. "You want more?"

At this moment, like another guest in the house, something in the pot came to a boil. A magical smell of chicken spread in the kitchen. This was the chicken soup with chicken to put on their plates later with boiled potatoes and carrots. Parsley was draped over everything; it had to be lifted off to get to the chicken.

Mama turned to look. Ellen looked. The guest turned around too with a new expression as though bread and butter had revived old feelings about what goes on in kitchens, how ordinary to eat every evening in the same place.

Suddenly he leaned back in his chair, shoved the plate away, put his face in his hands. He was really crying with the new strength he'd acquired.

"Mister, mister," said Mama coming close touching him on the shoulder as if overcoming a taboo. "Why are you crying? My god, why? You just had something to eat. Are you still hungry? Do you want something else?" She contemplated him.

The little man sobbed and let tears run between his fingers.

"He needs a hanky. He needs a hanky," Ellen sang out.

Her mother looked at her sharply. "All right. Take one out of the drawer. Go."

Ellen went to the exact place her mother meant, took a big folded handkerchief that belonged to her father. Running back she let it fly open like a kite holding it by a corner. "Here," she said.

Without looking he reached and blew his nose. He was making himself at home, thought Ellen. Would he move in? She settled down to wait and see. He didn't have a suitcase, and so far no name, either. Grown people were also known by who they were like, mother, father, uncle, cousin. Which would he be? Maybe an uncle. He'd be better than the ones she already had. But she'd never seen any of her uncles cry, or not have his own handkerchief. A sample of a strange faraway part of the world had strayed into their house.

"Poor man," said Mama.

"Don't talk to me that way," he said. "My heart is full of riches."

"Sure," said Mama, mocking him. "Look at the rich man. Look at him eating a stranger's food."

"It's my right," he said mildly like a comment on the spring sunshine.

He was making himself at home. A small quarrel can help make anybody feel at home.

"What's your name?" Ellen inserted herself into the goings-on.

"My name? I have no name. I am the messiah." He sat up straight and tore the hat off his head. On top was a small bald spot. The rest of his hair streamed downward, flat, dark, glistening, merging with his beard.

"Is that so?" said Mama. "Sooner or later I knew the messiah would come. Be welcome to our house," she said. "Let me help you take off your jacket. Make yourself at home. You'll eat supper with us maybe?"

He got up, took off his jacket uncovering a shirt with a tattered collar buttoned to his neck. He hung the jacket on the back of his chair, sat down again, by now completely at home.

Just then somebody else came to the back door. Without looking, Ellen knew who it was. Five minutes before, the newspaper boy had thrown the rolled-up *Daily News* onto the porch where papa stooped to pick it up before he came in.

"Who's coming?" said the guest.

"You're afraid?" said Mama. "The Cheka is looking for you?"

"What would the Cheka do with the messiah on their hands?"

Papa unlocked the door. Had her mother locked it after the messiah came in? "Good evening, ladies," said Papa, sweeping his hat in a theatrical gesture. In the middle of the sweep he stopped as he saw somebody at the kitchen table. "A guest?" he said, looking curiously.

"Yes, a guest," said Mama. "Guess who came to the door a little while ago? Him." She pointed. "He's hungry."

"Me," said Papa, "I thought I worked to feed three people. Now all of a sudden it's four. And who may you be *gospodin?*"

The guest was irritated. "I said it before. The messiah. You weren't expecting me? Doesn't everybody expect me?"

"If you were the messiah, I would be expecting you," said Papa. "But not so soon. Personally," he went on as he went through the kitchen on his way to hang up his coat and hat, "I would know right away. Nobody would have to say to me, 'Look, I'm the messiah.' You have a passport?"

"Passport?" said the guest. "It's America. No more passports. It's not the old country. The Czar, I hear, was shot."

"Ah ha," said Papa, "if you are the messiah, how do you know about such things—about passports in America, in Europe? He's a faker." He turned to Mama who was watching as she stirred vegetables into the pot.

The guest could hardly keep his attention on Papa, who kept on badgering him because he was watching the pot too, transformed. The bread he'd eaten must have awakened a dormant appetite.

It was time for supper. If not for the guest, Mama would be telling Ellen to set the table. Today without being told she put her schoolbooks away, came back and began to set out plates and silverware on the table in the dining room which was next to the kitchen. How many plates should she set? She looked at her mother from the kitchen doorway. But her mother was looking at her father as though herself trying to figure out what to do without asking in so many words.

Papa saw, but only shrugged, then sat down. No help there for Ellen. She decided for herself. Four.

"Even a messiah," her father was saying, "has to come from somewhere. You come from where?"

The guest smiled radiantly. "I don't remember."

"Don't lie to me," said Papa, "or I'll throw you out of my house. How can a man not know where he comes from?" He was angry. He got up, shook the guest by the shoulder. "Even the messiah comes from a place."

The guest, who hadn't stopped gazing at the pot containing the chicken burbling on the stove, was having trouble keeping his mind on Papa's questions. He said, "Don't bother me. Am I asking you?"

"I'll tell you if you ask me," said Papa with a righteous air.

"What do I need to know? Maybe I should go," he said without heart. Was he waiting for somebody to say, stay, eat with us?

"Stay. Eat with us." Mama said it. She was having trouble, too. She couldn't keep from looking at the stranger.

"With pleasure, madame." He got up, made a small bow and remained standing as though waiting to be directed to the table.

"Sit down. It's not quite ready."

Papa left the kitchen with an exasperated wave of his hand. Nobody said anything. Ellen went to write a few more lines of homework on a sheet of lined paper. The guest sat, patient, hands folded in front of him. Peace in the kitchen.

After awhile Mama said to Ellen, "Go call your father. It's ready."

She found her father sorting out his papers on the seat of the living room sofa. "It's ready. Fine." He left his papers and together they went back to the dining room. The guest was seated at the dining room table, his hands folded in his lap again, at the place Ellen had set for him.

"So, messiah, we welcome you to our house," said Papa.

"You want a prayer maybe?"

"We have a secular household," said Papa. "Prayer does nothing."

"Infidel," the guest said with venom.

"Suit yourself."

"Peace, peace," said Mama. She served the guest first as was fitting. His soup plate was so full another drop would have made it overflow. After she'd filled the other soup plates, Mama went to the kitchen and soon came back holding an oval platter on which lay the chicken. By then the guest had slurped up his soup. Ellen watched, thinking she'd never get away with slurping like that.

Papa smiled sadly. "A hungry man, this messiah."

"You like the soup?" Mama said. Easy to see she was pleased to see his appetite. She patted his hand.

"A question?" the guest barely stopped even for this short answer. He went on eating. Everybody else had finished: he kept on eating, systematically working his way across his plate: chicken, potatoes, more chicken, sliced carrots, a bite of bread.

Papa awoke from a spell of thought. *"Godspodin,"* he called out, "listen to me. I have a question. All the while you are here in my house I am thinking, what is the messiah doing here, with me, my fine wife"—he waved to Mama across the table—"my daughter, as smart as a boy."

"Why?" said Ellen.

Nobody paid attention. It was still Papa's turn to speak. "After all, it's not the old country any more. We are far from the place of *pogroms*. Here nobody hurts us."

The messiah held up a greasy finger and said, "Nobody? For sure?"

"Well," said Papa, "maybe not altogether. But it is no more the same thing. We're free. We can do what we want." He paused, then added, "Again, almost. What do we need a messiah for?"

The guest was more interested in what was left on his plate.

Papa went on. "All right, this is established. Even so we are in exile here as we were over there. But nobody rides through the street, his hand upraised looking for Jews."

"So?" said the messiah.

"Then what do we need the messiah for?"

"You mean he's out of work?" said Ellen.

Papa roared with laughter. "I told you, as smart as a boy." He stopped laughing. "We expect the messiah when we open the door, at the time for Jews to be delivered. Now is not the time."

"Uh huh," said the messiah as if he'd known about this all along. "What's a man to do?"

"Your services are no longer required. At least for the time being."

The messiah, who was now chewing a drumstick, managed a wicked smile. He set the drumstick down, wiped his hands and after a deep breath said, "A fine dinner, madame. I am grateful."

"You've lost your trade," said Papa. "What kind of future do you have in this world?"

He shrugged. The subject did not appear to interest him. "Do I know the answer?" He set down his fork and knife and leaned back, replete. "Ah," he said, patting his belly. "A blessing on you, madame."

Nobody had to tell Ellen it was time to remove the dishes. She piled up the plates with their chicken bones and silverware.

With no warning, the guest shot up, looking taller than before. He said, "Please," and helped clear the table.

"You're a guest," said Mama. "Sit down."

He barely acknowledged this and went on with his work. When it came time to wash dishes, he elbowed Mama out of the way, took a pair of uneven wire-rimmed glasses from a mysterious place in his clothes, perched them on his nose and with a dish towel around his enlarged waist, washed dishes.

"Look," said Mama. "Somebody who wants to wash dishes. A miracle."

Papa came to look at the miracle. "So," he said, skeptical. "Is it a miracle when a guest has the good idea of paying for his food with his labor?"

With her hands under her apron Mama stood watching, not so much as telling him how she liked dishes to be washed. "A fine man, no?" She looked for confirmation at Papa.

"I don't know if he's the messiah," said Papa. "But he's not a parasite. He works for his bread."

With this he went back to the living room to work on his papers. All evening he kept away from his desk in the dining room.

Like she was watching a movie, Ellen knew it was getting close to the end. Now that the messiah had finished, even hanging up the damp dish towel after drying the dishes, would he take his jacket from the kitchen chair, put it on, say goodbye and go? Where would he go? As a matter of fact, where did he come from?

All this must have come to him too at the same moment. He turned around, rubbed his hands, back to the sink, and looked at Mama. Something in his expression made Mama rip off her apron and start for the dining room, a sign that she didn't want more discussion. Then she stopped, turned back and said, "You have a place to go?"

"My place is with my friends," he said. Was he going to cry again? Did he still have Papa's handkerchief?

"You didn't answer," said Ellen.

"Sh," said her mother. "Go practice the piano."

"I can't. Papa's in the living room." Anyway, she wanted to see what was going to happen.

"You could say that you recognize in me the brother you left behind."

"My brothers are all here in America," she said.

"Or let me be your lost lover, the dark-haired boy you used to watch from a distance in your village. My name was David. You couldn't keep your eyes off me."

Mama flushed. "Is this a way for the messiah to talk? You're not the messiah. You're some kind of wanderer who makes up stories."

The messiah chuckled. "Stories? I'll tell you stories, all you want."

So he didn't put on his jacket and leave. By then it was dark, besides. After Papa finished with his papers in the living room, that was where the visitor slept that night: on the sofa. Papa transferred his papers back to his desk.

The next day it turned out that he knew how to use a vacuum cleaner, how to pass a mop on the edges of floor surrounding carpets and even how to operate the mangle to iron clothes in the basement. He folded all the sheets and towels and carried them up the backstairs in an awesome pile.

When Ellen came home the next day from school, she found her mother and the messiah at the kitchen table. He had settled on being a teller of stories and was telling Mama a story in a singsong voice making gestures with his hands.

Mama was listening and paid no attention to Ellen when she came in. "It can't be like that," she was saying to him. "Such a story, a fine story." As Ellen went through the kitchen, the messiah was beginning another story, the afternoon sun was coming in through the window.

After awhile she came back to stand in the doorway and listen too.

That's how the messiah came to their house. Now nobody else should expect him.

Crossing
for Marcella

MIRIAM McCLUNEY

In the rear seat of an old Studebaker sedan
we crossed the Mojave from Barstow in August 1945
five females huddled like smothered birds
my three sisters with our mother
who withdrew into a corner, always silent
sometimes nursing. The trip was hotter
than the war and maybe crueler—at least for us.
Father drove. A stern giant up front
who cursed our ailing grandfather beside him,
black market tires gone bad, steaming radiators,
our fatigue, and the infant's cry. This move
to New Mexico and that infant were new in our lives,
both intrusions to our childhood. She lay diaper-naked
in a wicker basket crossways to the door.
We became reluctant, miniature mothers
taking turns fanning her body, dripping water
across her forehead and lips. With dry, scared voices
we sang camp songs—"White Coral Belles,"
"Jacob's Ladder"—hoping for her to sleep. When she did
we took turns curling in our mother's lap. She held us
only to make space. Now each summer we all gather
for our youngest sister's birthday, retell the story
about the time we three sisters saved her life
crossing the desert—glad for the celebration,
watching our aged mother silent on the edge.

Rituals

MIRIAM McCLUNEY

Every winter laden with axes, hatchets,
down jackets and woolen caps
we leave for Mt. Taylor, piñon Christmas trees
and Zuni Shalako on our minds. Five trees
we cut for sisters, cousins, sons
leave brush trails in snow from dragging
pine behind, load our pickups and drive south
to Zuni along State 53 that bends and bends again
into those sacred mountains.

Our all night vigil begins at dusk as we trail down
narrow, earthen streets pass hornos and scattered farolitos
to river edge where we await the clacking Shalako.
We huddle together against the freezing night,
bundled close like trees we've cut. Suddenly with a dying sun,
ten foot giants appear along the river bank,
Macaw, raven, eagle feathered and turquoise faced
six huge heads clatter wooden beaks
into the unstill night.

"Spirits from the Dead," "Rain God Couriers," "Holy Messengers,"
"Kachinas"—our stumbling words unsure. Through village streets
we trail behind one towering figure led by pueblo wise men
and watch the Zunis throw cornmeal for good luck. We peer
through breath-fogged panes into the blessing of a house:
hear chanters, watch the kirtled Shalako bow and sway
as Mudheads, Longhorns dance until the rise of sun.

We sleep awhile
then journey home into our own unworldly magic
where we unpack the wooden manger scene,
place the star of wise men atop our fresh-cut tree,
decorate with ojos and corn necklaces,
and wonder if our christ-kachina
also comes across the darkened outskirt hills
to wander along the Zuni riverbank.

We Must Call a Meeting

JOY HARJO

I am fragile, a piece of pottery smoked from fire
                              made of dung,
the design drawn from nightmares. I am an arrow, painted
                              with lightning
to seek the way to the name of the enemy,
                    but the arrow has now created
its own language.
              It is a language of lizards and storms, and we have
begun to hold conversations
                    long into the night.
                                        I forget to eat
I don't work. My children are hungry and the animals who live
in the backyard are starving.
                    I begin to draw maps of stars.
The spirits of old and new ancestors perch on my shoulders.
I make prayers of clear stone
                    of feathers from birds
                              who live closest to the gods.
The voice of the stone is born
                    of a meeting of yellow birds
who circle the ashes of a smoldering volcano.
                    The feathers sweep the prayers up
and away.
         I, too, try to fly but get caught in the crossfire of signals
                    and my spirit drops back down to earth.
I am lost; I am looking for you
         who can help me walk this thin line between the breathing
                              and the dead.
You are the curled serpent in the pottery of nightmares.
You are the dreaming animal who paces back and forth in my head.

We must call a meeting.
                        Give me back my language and build a house
inside it.
          A house of madness.
                  A house for the dead who are not dead.
And the spiral of the sky above it.
And the sun
              and the moon.
                        And the stars to guide us called promise.

Witness

JOY HARJO

Ten years after they discovered her decomposed body in the fields near her husband's pueblo I walk the streets of a town in Italy. At night the walls of the amphitheatre flutter with shadows of lions and Christians. The four gates of power appear languid as off-duty angels. We can walk through walls eventually by faith and could all along, as misty forms passing through myths no one would ever believe: the tragic heroine becomes the trickster caught in the circle of obscenity becomes the woman who after pulling in her laundry from a window, adjusts her bra strap. It is the only gesture in the world. Every street leads to the center of town, which is an imaginary house with a table set for fools. The newly dead lean at the windows, listening to the clatter of knives and forks, the talk of ordinary things: who will weed the garden, a cousin's second wedding, until their own amazing story rattles the windows, sets them free. This is why they weep, and are who we mistake for the wind when we are grabbing at the blankets sliding into waves of the dark. No lover can suspend that knowledge, though it's possible to fly off together. We approached the tower sheltered by perpetual oaks. The Guinigi family will disappear if the magic isn't watered, so the roots are soaked and water makes a pool at my feet, or is it the shadow of a woman on the run? Italy and Isleta are as close as two eyes on the face of death. What was the last word she heard as she put her ear to the ground to run shoulder first into the earth, the place corn spirits hang out? Did they surround her, the woman who honored corn, but served the spirit of absolute truth in a world slowly severed by a dull knife? The stars were witness. I have seen them above us as sisters, her escort to another life, though tragedy would place them behind an eclipsed moon searching the alleys for scraps of food. Who was her midwife in the translation to honored food for the fields, to liquid skies over the pueblo, then the lights of Albuquerque in the distance of trains? It was in the spring when they found her, the earth stirring with the memory of the thousands of springs since the original fire whose ashes made clay. Turquoise was stripped from her ears. I can smell spring everywhere, my leg bones sticks for beans that will be planted and watered by faith. It was during the revolution, a night like this one when you can put your arms over the shoulders of the closest stars and laugh together. The moon wore a Stetson of water. Someone we loved had lost hope and smashed their car into a wall that wasn't there. The reports said they were drinking. Bitterness appeared to be free, and I nearly lost it myself a few times in the days of the angry count. We were driving the backroads around Albuquerque, the radio on country and a six-pack. It wasn't me flipping the tabs as we traded one word jokes in Navajo, but I have told the story so often that I will always ride with her in the careening truck. Soon there were sirens, turning lights and she pulled to a stop at the side of the road. Damn, the cops. Rolled down the window, wailing Jennings* tearing up the cab. They cited her for weaving! (She came from a family renowned for weaving.) We laughed and laughed. And the laughter resurrectd the lost ones two-stepping in the Bandbox Bar, where we had danced those nights we thought we had lost everything, heard the stabbings outside the door. Around midnight the puppet-maker appears exactly in time, in a room of whitewashed adobe, the only light on in Lucca. He thinks no one is watching as he dances with a puppet who is the memory of a lover he once walked the street with as a voyeur of the infinitely beautiful. An Italian libretto provides the curve. The walls constructed for defense around the town turn to grass. He laughs and cries to himself, remembering everything.

*Waylon Jennings first appeared this way in a poem by Gloria Emerson, Navajo writer.

Belated Visit

DAVID RAY

A week with mother, like staring at a shell-eyed god—
that gleaming abalone that takes in nothing,
iridescent, reflecting, indifferent as the sea.
It should, then, be an easy meditation to understand
at last what all your life's sickness has been,
grief generated by her grief. For it was she
Who taught you disappointment as a way of life,
As if woe were to be worshipped—she who still
Expects nothing after decades of nothing,
She you still hope to please though you know
She is unpleasable, unappeasable—she
For whom life is a crossword, a maze of words
That caged her always, never led out to the new
Life or a good man. Three times she crawled
On her knees to the desert, fled bloodied back
Into the valley of thorns. It is the blankness
Of those eyes that still scare you. Those nights
You longed for her are now part of limestone,
Buried deep, yet you recall them every time
You seek out the old eyes lidded in, almost sealed now.
Freud was right—everything comes out of the mind,
Even the swirling cosmos, the stars and the night wind.
All is metaphor. The next to last day you drive
Into a ditch. The last day you run out of gas.
And you know that even if you should achieve sainthood
She is still, in this life, not the one to discuss
Anything with. Sadly, that is true right up to brink
Of the grave, whichever of you stands there—
Whichever of you lies there, whichever of you
Despite himself or herself grieves there.

And then at week's end she does what she was good at
In those days—flies away, leaving you gazing after,
feeling the hurt. As a child you could not say
quite what hurt so deep. Now you can say. And stay
Where cactus blooms—so welcome for its lack
Of pretense. It never pretended to love,
never promised a thing. *Poveretta,*
who could not love me. *Poveretta,*
whom I cannot love, whose eyes haunt me still.

The Fire-bird

HARVENA RICHTER

There was a fire-bird who lived in an ice cave high in the mountains of Nepal. It had appeared in early legends, in the Book of Books, and people thought of it as westerners think of unicorns. It was a delightful idea—what really *was* a fire-bird? And many paintings of the fabled creature appeared on silk and rice paper and heavy linen. It was portrayed as a bird whose every feather shot forth fire; the crest on its head was a flamboyant torch.

Its beauty was so compelling that artisans tried to capture it in replica. They traded all over the world for feathers that looked like flames. Moguls waited years for their own fire-bird to be completed, the claws fashioned cleverly from rubies. Such a fire-bird was kept in a cage with bars of golden wire.

And so the fire-bird existed on the edge of reality, but never within it. Treatises were written about the ice cave where it lived—a cave that never melted from the heat of the flames. Water should put out fire; they were ancient enemies. The philosophers discovered, therefore, a world in which the elements never warred—air and earth, water and fire. It bespoke of the falseness of dualities. Harmony bound opposites into a perfect whole.

It happened one day that Sherpas, looking for a leopard who had killed a young woman, found the ice cave with the fire-bird. It lifted its claws delicately, up and down. Its plumes rustled with the hiss of flames. The Sherpas warmed their hands at the heat radiating from the niche whose frozen walls gave back reflections running from palest rose to wine-dark red. They observed that the walls did not drip water, that no stream splashed down from the cave to the rocks below.

When they told the priests, it was explained that they had seen a vision. That part of the mountain they described was well travelled. Nothing strange had ever been recorded there. That it approximated the vision in the Book of Books only confirmed the priests' conclusions.

An avalanche sealed off that particular valley for several centuries. It was only when a climbing expedition, armed with pitons, ropes, and two unwilling Sherpas, climbed the rocky barrier that the valley was entered once again. One of the Alpinists, sensing a strange glow, turned and saw the fire-bird in its niche of ice.

There began a steady stream of visitors—travellers who didn't mind the high altitude, a few intrepid reporters, a stream of devout Sherpas. The priests did not appear. It was thought they could not deal with what had happened at Monabba Pass. Many photographs, colored and black-and-white, were taken, but when developed, remained blank. So did the numerous reels of film. It only convinced the priests that what was happening was a sustained vision which was nonetheless erroneous.

The country's president—for the moguls had long since vanished with their fire-birds in golden cages—was disturbed by the fuss about the fire-bird. He himself, with three bodyguards and a small army division following at a discreet distance, went to visit the fire-bird in its cave of ice. When he returned to his estate, encompassed by four successive walls, he was greatly shaken. He ordered a scientific investigation, and the best biologists in the country, and two from the western world, went to examine the fire-bird and draw conclusions. With asbestos gloves they pulled the creature from its niche, measured the claws, the feathers, felt the beating of its heart.

When the devout came the next day they discovered only a mound of black ashes. FIRE-BIRD DESTROYED blared the newspaper headlines. An enemy, the account continued, had penetrated the guard posted on the trail.

Further editions of dictionaries, encyclopedias, and histories expunged the story of the fire-bird at Monabba Pass. It is still found in folk tales, and the Book of Books. And occasionally, in small curio shops catering to the western trade, there are fire-birds for sale made of papier-mâché.

Tres Copas de Chanate Black and Sweet

LEVI ROMERO

órale ese
saludes de south fourth
spicy street overflowing with
creamy joy and scornful sorrow
resembling a faded watercolor painting
rotting under the sun
growing tangled 'neath the billboard
bosom sighs of a new frontier

I have felt you waking up sweating
to the sounds of 3 a.m. trains
rolling in on greasy tracks
spreading across your innocence
like melting butter on a hot tortilla

your gold toothed mouth of prominence
has gone silent under the weight
of rusted steel and faded brick
where cash registers once sang
like Christmas chimes

on your black heeled streets
bleed tattooed backs in blue ink
penance for your soul
proud puro Barelas 13

your chapped dusty sidewalks
kissing the calloused souls
of homeless saints
popping out of trash bins
in the red eyed dawn
are fed by the black vein freeways
dripping diseased America
into your dirt alley dreams

your complaints become rheumatoid groans
of aching feet sliding across linoleum
floors towards clock radios weeping
mexican ballads into the trumpet gold
haze of memories too strong to stick
or sink into the Río Grande mud
me llamo Manuel Leyba
but they call me manual labor

behind the soot screen windows
and padlocked doors of the Redball Cafe
sit chrome and metalflake countertops
frozen in the chewy silence
of a catholic Sunday ringing sad
a billion more still yearn
to be served

pick-up trucks once danced
into the Royal Fork restaurant
from Gallup and Farmington
slipping through the honeydew
sweetness of ripening September

Oh, earth goddess
of asphalt and grime
let me hear your hearty laugh
flapping heavy like El Cambio's
storefront window ads
that fill my salty visions
with sweet roll promises
crumbling onto the dry
tongue of my worn out shoes

Los Heroes

LEVI ROMERO

los watchavamos
cuando   pasaban
echando jumito azul
en sus ranflas aplanadas
como ranas
de ojelata

eran en los dias
de los heroes

cuando habia heroes
turriqiando en
lengua mocha
y riza torcida

Q-volé

ahora nomas   pasan
los recuerdos
uno atras de el otro
y mi corazon
baila

bendicion

bendicion es
estar contento

Señor gracias por . . .

gracias por
todo

Sombras de la Jicarita

GABRIEL MELENDEZ

La Jicarita Peak, twelve thousand feet in the air; *xumatl*, the sky bowl of our indomitable spirit.

La cumbre de la Jicarita, doce mil pies sobre el nivel de mar; *xumatl*, el jumate celeste de nuestro espíritu indomable.

I

Most certainly, we have never thought to discard the litany of souls that surrounds each person born at the foot of La Jicarita Peak, nor can we neglect the accompanying clamor of a multitude of faceless and anonymous voices that impregnate the very air we breathe and are with us at each moment of the day and of the night. Now, they are the unseen visitors that sit at our kitchen tables when we speak of the past; now, the ancestral countenance that we believe we've recognized on the faces of strangers that we pass on the street; now, the elongated shadows that move in the old abandoned patios; now, the unearthed bones that walk the earth and do not know eternal rest or peace.

* * *

Lo cierto es que nunca hemos pensado deshacernos de esta letanía de ánimas que envuelve la mirada de cuanta persona ha nacido al pie de la Jicarita, ni hemos podido desatender de esta multitud sonorosa de voces anónimas y sin rostro que enpapa hasta el aire que respiramos y nos acompaña a cada hora del día y de la noche. Ahora, son las invisibles visitas que rodean la mesa de nuestras cocinas cuando nos sentamos a platicar del pasado; ahora, los perfiles ancestrales que creimos reconocer en los desconocidos que pasamos en la calle; ahora, las elongadas sombras que se mueven en los destartalados patios de casas abandonadas; ahora, los huesos descubiertos que andan sobre la tierra sin paz y sin eterno descanso.

II

In late summer, rain clouds thicken quickly on the ridge-line of the sierra and the distant rumble of their thunder echos endlessly in the mountain canyons and in the tall stands of spruce until, like the water in the river, the sound ebbs its way out to the open llanos to the east. As the Valley fills with a gray light as might be reflected from great mirrored hallways, the animals feel the air tingle across their spines: yellow house cats jump suddenly from the windowsills lined with coffee cans potted with geraniums; village dogs creep under the porch steps or find the last dark corner of the storeroom to hide from the storm; young mares and stallions race along the pasture lands to the river bank, their nostrils flaring, their manes flying in the air, the mirrored image of the fields caught in the obsidian light of their oblong vision. Fire dances everywhere on the mountain and lightning cracks the sky. The mountain's fire flashes blue-white knife blades through the crisp air above the deep green of the scrub oak.

This kind of lightning has broken the back of prize bulls grazing in the high pastures, leaving their carcasses bowed and bloated in the middle of boggy meadows; it has split open the massive trunks of conifer trees and left the forest smoldering from blackened wounds in the earth; it has caught unfortunate stockmen crossing barbed wire fences on their way to shelter and left them dangling there like fish on a trout line. The rising waters of the downpours that follow, rushing down the mountain, have swept away young calves, have cut apple orchards and beanfields in two; have washed away bridges lifting them like tiny wooden boats on the swell of their crested muddy waters and have snuffed out the life's breath of infant children caught with their parents midstream in old model-T Fords. The memory of such mishap is held in the gaze of the old people of the Valley like the yellowed news clippings of defunct newspapers pressed into the pages of family Bibles. The old people have known the delicate dance of the earth's elements: wind, fire, and water. They've seen the changing masks of life and death, and death and life, on the face of each new day's horizon. When the storms appear, and the fury of the mountain sounds, the old women step out in the rushing wind, their long grey hair filled with electricity, and they cut at the clouds with long kitchen knives and cast salt to the four directions of the wind and they chant the song of lives upon lives of endless memory: "Santa Bárbara doncella, líbranos del rayo de la centella." Then the flashing light and the wind-blown shadows of the clouds dance about the fields and above the rusted tin roofs of the village and through the cottonwoods along the river, flashing off window panes recessed deep in timeless adobe walls. Many people swear to have seen the shadows of the dead in this half light, moving through the open doorways of the old abandoned houses, walking silently behind the tongued flames of oil lamps into the inner rooms where they are lost from sight. Are they dancing in the dark? Are they praying at their altars in the dim glow of candles? Are they covering the mirrors with black cloths to draw away the lightning? Are they the half clothed bony skeletons of lovers, locked in loving embraces awaiting their turn at life again?

* * *

En los últimos días del verano, las nubes de lluvia se tupan en las cumbres de la sierra y el rodar de sus truenos hace un echo interminable en los cañónes de la montaña y entre los altos pinavetes, hasta que como el agua en el río, su sonido se mengua en dirección a los llanos abiertos del Este. Al llenarse el valle con una luz gris como el que podía darse por el reflejo de los espejos de enormes salas, los animales sienten el aire cargado cosquillarles el espinazo: los gatos saltan de repente desde las ventanas colmadas con geranios en latas de café; los perros del pueblo se meten debajo de las escaleras de los portales o encuentran donde esconderse de la tormenta en el último lugar oscuro de la despensa; las potrancas y los potros galopan por los campos de pasturas hasta la ribera del río, sus narices se abren, sus crines se desparraman en el aire, la imagen reflejada de los campos se fija en la luz de pedernal de sus ojos oblicuos. La lumbre baila en toda parte de la montaña y los relámpagos cuartean los cielos. La montaña destella navajazos de luz plomiza que cortan el aire fresco sobre el verde oscuro del sabinal.

Son centellas de las que han roto los espinazos de toros finos pasteando en la sierra, dejando sus bultos pandeados e hinchados en medio de prados lodosos, o que han partido los gruesos troncos de los pinorreales y han dejado el bosque chamuscado y humeante de heridas negras en la tierra; o han alcanzado a ganaderos cruzando cercos de alambre en busca de repecho y los ha dejado tendidos ahí como truchas prendidos de un anzuelo. Las crecientes de aguas que en seguida buscan su descenso de la montaña, se han llevado terneras y han cortado por la mitad arboledas y milpas; se han llevado puentes, alzándolos en la creciente de sus aguas revoltosas como barquitos de niños; han arrebatado el resuello de vida de niños en brazos, presos con sus padres a mitad de una corriente en viejos carros Ford, Model T. La memoria de un sin número de semejantes atrasos está grabada en los recuerdos de los ancianos como si fueran los recortes amarillentos de periódicos desbalagados que se han guardado entre las hojas de la Biblia de la casa.

Los ancianos conocen el baile delicado de los elementos de la tierra: viento, lumbre y agua. Han visto cambiarse las máscaras de la vida y la muerte, y de la muerte y la vida sobre el horizonte de la madrugada. Cuando aparecen las tormentas y la furia de la montaña se anuncia, las viejitas salen al viento recio, sus mechas de cabello gris llenándose de electricidad y cortan las nubes con cuchillos largos y echan sal a las cuatro direcciones del viento y cantan la canción de vidas sobre vidas de memorias sin fin: "Santa Bárbara doncella, líbranos del rayo de la centella." Y entonces el destello de la luz y las sombras acarreadas por el viento se baten y danzan entre los campos, y sobre los techos oxidiados del pueblo, y entre los álamos del río, y relampaguen en bastidores, enmarcados en antiquísimas paredes de adobe. Mucha gente jura haber visto las sombras de los muertos en esta tenebrosa luz, sombras que se mueven en las puertas de destartaladas casas de adobe, caminando silenciosamente detrás de la luz de faroles de aciete, internándose en los últimos cuartos donde se pierden de vista. ¿Estarán bailando en la oscuridad? ¿Estarán rezando ante sus altares en la debil luz de velas antiguas? ¿Estarán tapando los espejos con mantas negras para ahuyentar los relámpagos? ¿Serán esqueletos con los pechos desnudos, asidos como amantes en un abarzo de amor esperando su retorno a la vida?

III

Oh, I think it was about one-thirty, just after the noon hour, and when I got up to put away the dishes the washcloth fell from my hand and I thought to myself, surely someone is going to visit me. Well, ten minutes hadn't gone by when I heard a knock, first at the window and then later at the screen door. I looked out, but I saw nothing. I suppose the neighbor here is nailing a board or something around by his house, I thought, and I even called out, "Hey, friend, what the devil are you up to?" and since I didn't hear anyone answer me, I sat down again and picked up a book I have here about Vicente Silva's gang of bandits and then, again, after only a short time I heard a knock, but this time it was very loud and I heard what sounded like rocks rolling off the tin roof and, by God, just then the screen door opened wide and I felt a cold chill in the air and that's when I saw her. There was no doubt about it. It was my comadre Petra, just as she had been in life, though not old as she had become in recent years. It was Petra as she was when we were young and her eyes would fill with fire. And I heard her call out in a very low and serene voice as if she were very far away, "Ay, dear one, the joy of my youth." Because, you know, my comadre Petra loved me very deeply. Now I'm sure she came that afternoon to take her leave because she had never forgotten me. They say that she would cry as if her heart were about to burst when I was first sent to the war in France. And when I came back and they had already married her to the now deceased Don Benito Sánchez, what could be done? But she often thought of me and never forgot the time we had as lovers. Oh yes, I knew her as a man knows a woman way before Don Benito and as the song goes, "Oh what times those were my friend, Señor Simón." We shared nights when we wouldn't sleep and we would romp in bed like wolves in heat until the first light of day scratched the sky. It must be as they say, my friend; the blood is known to boil, the blood is known to boil. The next day after Petra's visit, my cousin Evaristo Trujillo came to tell me that Petra had died over in Las Golondrinas that previous afternoon and that she had been in agony for a long time. Evaristo took it upon himself to let me know because having attended to her in the last hours, he had heard her call out, "Ay, Manuel, my dear one, the joy of my youth!" Oh yes my friend, that's exactly how these things are.

* * *

O yo creo que sería como la una y media, por a'i, poco después de mediodía y cuando me levanté a alzar los trastes se me cayó el estropajo y dije entre mí, seguro que me va a llegar una visita. Pues, no habían pasa'o diez minutos cuando oí tocar, primero a la ventana y luego al ratito a la puerta de alambre. Me asomé, pero no vide nada. Quizás el vecino anda clavando alguna tabla aquí al la'o, pensé y hasta le grité de la puerta: "Je, vecino, ¿qué diantres anda haciendo?" y como no oí que me respondiera naiden, me puse a le'r un libro que tengo a'i de la gavilla de Vicente Silva, cuando al rato, otra vez que oigo tocar a la puerta, pero esta vez bien fuerte y luego voy oyendo como pierdas rodando por encima del latón del techo y, por Dios Santo, se abrió la puerta bien abierta y sentí como un escalofrío en el aigre y antonces sí, la vide. Era ella, mi comadre Petra, lo mismo que era en vida, pero no como en estos últimos años cuando se hizo vieja. Era Petra igualito a cuando éranos jóvenes y sus ojos se llenaban de luz. Y oí su voz como muy quedita o desde muy lejos que me decía, "ay nito, niño de mis ojos." Porque me quería muncho mi comadre Petra. 'Hora estoy seguro que vino a despedirse porque nunca se había olvida'o de mí. Dicen que lloraba que parecía que se le iba a despedazar el corazón cuando primero me tuve que ir a la guerra en Francia. Y ya cuando volví de allá, ya la había casa'o con Benito Sánchez, ¿pues ya qué se le iba a hacer? pero se acordaba de mí, amigo y no dudo que sería por el tiempo que andábamos enamora'os. Si yo la conocí como un hombre conoce a una mujer muncho antes que el dijunto Benito y como dice la canción, "ay qué tiempos, señor don

Simón." Había noches que no dormíamos y retozábamos en la cama como lobos en celo hasta que rayaba el sol. Será por algo que dicen, la sangre hierbe, hermano, la sangre hierbe. Otro día, después de la visita de Petra, me vino a avisar mi primo Evaristo Trujillo que mi comadre Petra había muerto allá en las Golondrinas esa misma tarde y que había agoniza'o por muncho tiempo. El mismo, mi primo Evaristo, me vino a avisar porque, habiéndola acompaña'o en sus últimas horas, izque la Petra había dado voces en su delirio y izque dicía: "Ay, Manuel, nito, niño de mis ojos." Sí amigo, si asina son esas cosas.

Berkana

WILMA RODRIGUEZ

                      Wet adobe and
                        white clay
Scent the rippling heat
    for lost summer days
        when Abuela could shoo
            cats with
Slingshots and marbles
    like a walking shadow.
        Nowadays, new shadows
            cross the moon and
My world of gatos y crickets
    remains only as subtle as
        dried desert teas and the
            thought, *y volvere*.

The Pear Courtyard

DEBORAH MULDAVIN

I

Heavy eggshell bodies plop in the courtyard, grasshoppers
bright and infrequently falling
on brown leaves coursing seasons under the peartree.
The hollyhocks succumb, through whole to lacy leaves,
embellishing St. Joseph's impoverished staff, the stem,
with skeletal collars and the next—
fat buds grazed,
     opening necrotic petals.

Lilacs, elongated wild roses, cluster skyward,
flagstones stand briefly stripped of bindweed,
walls melt down, the greenery closes the sky.

The years are incidental and the occasional radiant plant, miraculous,
does not interfere with the fast growth of decay.

II

A wire girdles the tree crowned with kingbirds;
                   half of the branches are dead.
The wire, in family history, hooked Chinese lanterns
   pivoting in floral breeze carrying
      piano improvisations, the drying of paint
         on paper and the soft
swooshing movements of subsistence, paid to carry trays.

The tree and rock traceries are abandoned to resistance—
self reseeding hollyhocks, copper pennies
corroding between the flagstones
     the understory to rattlesnakes and kingsnakes.

III

Darkling beetles walk the adobe wing, as indifferently
as walking the shadowed side of a canyon.
Grown children with changed world views
                    seal out the squirrels from the house,
and pull themselves from overremembrance.

IV

The grasshoppers fall each summer, fatten, and go
to a life without leaves.

Balboa Park

DEBORAH MULDAVIN

I do not wish to re-enter the life of myself that I hear
on the telephone, my child crying with my missing her,
that I see in the smile of a boy, my missing him, at the zoo.

I walk alone on sandal footed legs under the rare skirt tenting
my legs walking, heels walking.

I pace my breath, lifting the coffee.
A man waits at the gate with a bucket of emptiness marked
by an occasional coin for the hungry

while I eat an avocado and crab omelette
a cat pads the Spanish tile and drops to a fountain,
drops a quick tongue that radiates seconds of pearl.

My careful breath pushes—
It is my vacation, a deserved rest
not to be disturbed by a homeless child who wants to burn the
    world down.
What else?
The omelette doesn't stick in my throat, paintings
still hang in museums with once and still wonderful brushstrokes.
As not myself, the price can be anything.

White Buffalo Woman

JEANE JACOBS

It was the month after the corn festival: the time of year the rolling hills looked their best, decorated in an array of orange, red, and yellow leaves. The wind blew in gusty intervals to loosen the leaves which would later fall to the ground.

White Buffalo Woman stood at the base of the hills enjoying the view of the setting sun's reflection off the changing leaves. She knew this was a good time to die and she had come a long way to do just that. She wasn't quite sure how old she was, maybe one-hundred-and-six or perhaps one-hundred-and-eight. She had raised many children, seven of her own and quite a few others who had lost their parents in one way or another.

Many years had gone by and she had forgotten many of the children's names and faces, but many generations of her own tribe, the Choctaw and some Cherokee, a few Shawnee and two white children would long remember White Buffalo Woman as the one who fed them and sang them to sleep at night.

White Buffalo Woman raised her walking stick toward the blue Mississippi sky. Her body ached with pain brought on by her long journey. She spoke out loud to the trees, the earth, and the sky: "Oh great Hashtalhi, give me the strength to stay alive long enough to reach the Nanih Waiya. I am an old woman and it is my time to die. I want to lay my weary bones on the mound of my ancestors. I will not trouble you for nothing else."

She dropped her arms to her sides and squatted in order to relieve some of the strain on her back. The wind whistled through the cedar trees. White Buffalo Woman felt as if someone was near. Maybe the wind spirits were trying to tell her something. "Speak to me. I am listening," she said.

The branches of the cedars rubbed together, making creaky noises. In the distant clear sky she noticed a golden brown hawk floating gracefully toward her. White Buffalo Woman turned her head to get a clear view of the gliding bird. There was something familiar about this hawk. It seemed larger than most of the hawks in this region.

"Ah ya eoki." She remembered long ago she knew a Kiowa woman called Winter Snow who had the spirit of a golden hawk.

The hawk came so close White Buffalo Woman could see the color of its eyes. It swooped back into the air, circling with one powerful wing movement then diving to the earth. The gold and brown spotted hawk flew between the cedar trees with delicate motions. It came to a silent perched position on a low branch near where White Buffalo Woman was sitting.

The hawk's gray-green eyes gazed into the dark black eyes of White Buffalo Woman, almost hypnotizing her. White Buffalo Woman sat on the soft earth as still as she could. She wondered what this magnificent bird wanted from her.

A strong gust of wind howled through the trees. In an instant the hawk had disappeared and a young girl with long thick dark hair stood facing White Buffalo Woman.

"I have come to help you on your journey. You are safe." The girl spoke softly as she squatted on the ground next to White Buffalo Woman.

"I am glad you have come. I was beginning to feel alone." White Buffalo Woman trusted the young girl with old eyes, immediately.

"I am called Montee. I am a descendant of Winter Snow of the Kiowa tribe and the great-granddaughter of Haloka. They have sent me here." Montee leaned toward White Buffalo Woman and stroked her coarse gray hair slowly.

White Buffalo Woman noticed Montee was wearing the clear hawk carved stone around her neck that Winter Snow once wore. "Yes, I remember Winter Snow and the Cherokee-Irish Medicine Woman, Haloka. They were my friends from a long ago time. How are they?"

"Winter Snow died before I was born. But I have seen her in my dreams many times. She is well and is looking forward to visiting with you." Montee smiled and her eyes looked upon White Buffalo Woman with great kindness. "Haloka and my Choctaw grandmother Nona are praying for our safety at this moment."

"Of course, Nona. She was one of my orphaned children long ago. I was there the day she married Haloka's son." White Buffalo Woman's eyes filled with tears. "I haven't thought of that day for many years. But I remember how beautiful Nona was. Her hair was coal black hanging down her back, like strands of a horse's mane. She was the strongest girl child I raised."

"She is still very strong." Montee stretched her shoulders back. She felt proud of her grandmother's strength.

"Eeyo. You are of many bloods," White Buffalo Woman said. "Must be you are the girl child Winter Snow spoke of many times. The one who would carry on her goodness."

"Truth. I am the one," Montee said. "You are White Buffalo Woman, the mother of many lost children." Montee stood up and placed her hand around the older woman's arm to help her to her feet.

"You know why I have made such a long journey?" White Buffalo Woman asked as she straightened her cotton print skirt.

Montee reached for the old one's bundle. "Yes."

The two women walked briskly along the edge of the Pearl River. Both of them knew they would soon reach a clearing where they could rest for the night, as the sunlight was fading quickly. White Buffalo Woman had to be silent while she walked. It seemed to take most of her breath just to keep the pace. Montee held her arm, which helped.

The woods around them were alive with the noises of animals and birds as the cool of the evening descended. Montee recognized the roar of a plane in the distant sky.

They would rest in the clearing for the night and resume their journey early in the morning, which would put them at the Nanih Waiya around noon.

The Nanih Waiya was a Choctaw word that meant "Leaning Hill," which described a large mound that rose some ninety feet above the trees with a natural ring of rocks around the top. The mound was located at a point where three rivers came together. The peak of the hill appeared as if it were leaning toward the largest river. Long ago the Choctaw built two smaller mounds at the foot of the Nanih Waiya. The first housed the bones of their dead and the second was used for ceremonies.

They reached the clearing with just enough daylight left to prepare their bedding and build a small fire to keep the chill off for awhile. White Buffalo Woman handed Montee a small piece of dried meat and divided the bag of corn into plastic cups.

"Thank you," Montee said, chewing the tough beef with her mouth open. "It is good. I had forgotten my hunger."

White Buffalo Woman nodded in agreement. She dumped half a cup of corn into her mouth and sprinkled some on the ground near the fire. "It will dry and the birds will have it for breakfast after we are gone," she said.

"We must rest now. Our walking will not be easy tomorrow," White Buffalo Woman said, and for a moment she felt as if she were mothering one of her many children.

"This is true," Montee said. "My grandmother told me of how you used to sing them to sleep when she was a child. Could you please sing me one song?" Even though she had turned sixteen her last birthday and had received her awakening, late at night she still enjoyed the kindness of the older women.

"Eyoki. That would please me greatly." White Buffalo Woman's voice was mellow and sweet as she sang a Choctaw lullaby. The words told the story about how the "little people" fell to the earth from the heavens to plant the flowers, how they had been taught to spin and weave by the bronze spider on their journey to earth so they could spin and weave many beds of flowers across the fields.

White Buffalo Woman's tender song faded with the glow of the fire. She gently pulled the wool blanket over Montee's shoulders and removed the loose strands of her hair from the girl's face. Slowly she lowered her tired body on the bed of leaves Montee had piled together for them to sleep on and covered herself, leaving her right arm on top of the blanket around Montee's waist.

It was almost noon when the two women reached the first mound, the mound of the dead. Their journey had been smooth, but they were both hungry. White Buffalo Woman had picked some mulberries along the way and that was all they had left to eat besides a small bit of corn they were saving.

"Well, we are here," White Buffalo Woman said, looking around at the vine covered mounds. "I wonder what happened to the caretaker of this place. I remember the last time I came here for the ceremony of the Ribbon Lady Dance this was a beautifully kept garden spot."

"He is still here, but he could use a few hired hands," Montee said as she sat on the ground, removing her soft leather moccasins and rubbing her feet. She moved closer to White Buffalo Woman. Without any hesitation White Buffalo Woman held her feet out to Montee. White Buffalo Woman sat quietly on the tree stump while Montee removed her brown moccasins and her white bobby socks and massaged her tired old feet.

Montee grinned a little at the socks. "It is very smart of you to wear such things on your feet," she laughed.

"Yes, I know. One of my many granddaughters gave them to me and she told me they were very popular. I like them." White Buffalo Woman smiled and turned her chin to the sky.

"I seen ya'uns for near an hour on the path," a graveled voice spoke from behind the trees.

Montee jumped to her feet. She turned to face the voice, her arms bent at the elbows and her hands open, palms facing each other, and her leg muscles clenched as in a wrestler's first position.

"Now, don't be gettin' frisky, girl. I ain't aimin' ta hurt ya none." The voice moved closer and a dark stocky man appeared between the shadows of the trees in the noon-day light. "My name be Neshoba. That ring a bell ta ya, woman?"

"Ugh, the caretaker," White Buffalo Woman said, feeling a bit angry that he interrupted her massage.

"Ah reckon y'all ain't come for no ceremony. The corn harvest is over and it be a month until the Dancin' Rabbit do'ins be here," Neshoba slurred out. Neshoba's hair was coarse and black, his skin a deep bronze. He had a wide nose which spread almost flat across his face. White Buffalo Woman had seen him before at the ceremonies she had attended. His father had been a great Choctaw hunter and had many wives but Neshoba's mother was not one of them. Neshoba's mother was a slave and had run away. His father captured her and had four children by her.

"Ah guessed what's ya was comin' here for, so the place is ready," Neshoba said gruffly and disappeared back into the trees.

Montee put White Buffalo Woman's white socks and moccasins back on her feet before she put her own moccasins on. The two women walked to the point where the three rivers came together and turned to face the Nanih Waiya. The leaning hill was a magnificent sight.

Montee gathered a pile of leaves and spread the wool blanket over it. "You rest here for awhile, White Buffalo Woman. I will search for something to eat."

Montee walked to the edge of the river and squatted to wash her face and hands. She smiled in the direction of White Buffalo Woman, who had already fallen asleep. Montee wandered into the woods until she came to a clearing similar to the one near her home.

She took a large stick and dragged it on the ground to form a circle in the dirt. She sat inside the circle and prayed. "Thank you, Great One. I am here to bring goodness to White Buffalo Woman's transition. Your guidance is all I ask."

A silver light shone directly over Montee's head, a reflection from the sun against the changing leaves. She sat still for some time listening to the sounds of the wind singing through the trees.

She walked back toward where she had left White Buffalo Woman sleeping and on the side of the path hanging between two cedar trees was a line with two catfish. She took her knife from the pouch on her belt and cut one of the fish away from the line. She took a small clump of tobacco and tied it to the line in exchange for the fish. She went to the river, skinned the long black fish clean then wrapped it in some wet leaves.

She gathered wood for a fire and cleaned sticks for a cooking rack. The two women enjoyed the large pieces of catfish and the few bits of corn that were left in the bag.

After they finished their meal Montee gathered more wood to keep the fire going. White Buffalo Woman told Montee stories of the past and sang for her again. The two of them slept as they had the night before.

Montee awakened with the weight of White Buffalo Woman's arm heavy around her waist. She suddenly realized that she didn't feel White Buffalo Woman's breath against her neck. Montee remembered dreaming of White Snow and White Buffalo Woman laughing and talking together.

Montee rolled out from under White Buffalo Woman's arm and, kneeling beside her lifeless body, she began to stroke her gray hair. She sang the lullaby of the little people as she softly pushed White Buffalo Woman's hair away from her face.

"Her place is ready," Neshoba's graveled voice came from the path. Beside him stood a tall, thin, light-skinned man with high cheek bones and black slits for eyes. Behind the two men stood a round woman with short cropped hair. She was dressed in men's clothing and held a pail of water.

"Y'all go fishin' or sumpin' for awhile. Us will take care of this magni'cent lady." The round woman pushed her way between the two men, who stood quietly for a second before they both shrugged their shoulders and walked away.

"Move over, girl. I'm called Rankin. My folks was what our people use to call the Bonepickers. 'Course us don't do it that ways no more. All us do now is take care of the burial ceremonies and such," she said as she wiped White Buffalo Woman's face with the wet cloth.

Montee watched every step of the preparation of the body as she sat on the ground, making the seven stakes for the Crossing Over ceremony.

The body was ready and from out of nowhere Neshoba and his skinny friend appeared with a travois. They lifted White Buffalo Woman up onto the travois and carried her to the burial place. They laid her on a low platform and covered her body with a fancy beaded blanket, leaving only her head showing.

Montee went alone to the river, washed herself, and dressed in the ceremonial garb given to her by Rankin. She folded her own clothing neatly and looked down at the white buckskin dress and white handmade moccasins that she wore. The dress had tiny white shells sewn in diamond designs across the top.

Montee parted her long hair in the middle and braided two braids, placing the two hawk feathers she kept in her medicine bundle in her right braid. She wrapped the quills with a leather string tightly. She felt like she was living in the long-ago times of her ancestors. She knew Winter Snow and White Buffalo Woman were proud of her.

When Montee reached the burial site there were several people waiting for her. Two men in traditional dress—one with a large tree drum—stood together. Several women with shawls over their heads stood outside the circle of the platform. Neshoba and Rankin approached Montee.

Rankin had changed into a cotton squaw dress, but her short hair and her harsh voice were still the same. "Ya bring the silver rings, girl?" she asked as she tucked a medicine pouch in Montee's hand. "Ya 'pose ta put that under her blanket. It holds things she'll need on her journey."

Montee nodded. She began to place the seven stakes in a semi-circle around the body with the tallest, seventh stake farthest to the west. It was believed that the happyland was in the west. Then she fastened silver rings with different colored ribbons to the top of each stake. The silver loops and stakes were designed to help the spirit pull itself from the earth and pointed in the direction of the happyland.

The drummer began beating the large drum victoriously and the singers chanted happy songs. The women chanted the funeral cry and danced in a semi-circle with one woman beside each stake to help the spirit start her journey.

The words of their chant told the story of the happiness White Buffalo Woman shared with many others. That there will be no sad songs sung for her, that, instead, there were many smiles left behind. Of how her company was enjoyed by those who loved her. The ceremony went on until after nightfall.

In the early morning light a feast was prepared and White Buffalo Woman's body was placed in the ground and covered over with dirt as prayers were said.

Montee pulled each stake out of the ground slowly as only one woman sang the happy song. She started with the tallest stake and moved around the semi-circle, dancing to signify that White Buffalo Woman had crossed over with a successful journey.

3 Songs of the Medicine Bundle

JAMES THOMAS STEVENS

Take me up in your hair
And I will teach you.
I'm dumping my bundle of tongues
On old earth.
You can speak—whichever—
You will choose.

Move your tongue bone
Back and forth.
Click—click—click.

I could heal you,
With language
And I refuse
To tell.

My bundle says to move
away the death of supernature.
Somewhere more powerful to lay
standing up.

Dreaming's difficult now
but
the bundle says to learn.

In the morning I bind
the bundle of heat—like that.
To the back of my round head
I tie knots.

Night undoes the bowcord—like that.
And my flathead
goes to sleep.

Medea in Taos

JAMES HOGGARD

No, the next morning she did not wake
to horror. *I didn't even go to bed,*
she said: *I was distracted but the fits
didn't start till later.* I must admit,
of course, I just knew her old, back when
she lived near here for several years.
Both noon and night she haunted La Fonda
and we'd often walk off time together.

Neither ragpicker nor rich, she always wore
a short-crowned, wide-brimmed green hat aslant
her brow to keep the sun's glare off her eyes
and hide the wrinkles that webbed her face.
But ghosts of beauty still lived wild in her,
made her recall the nights, those lyrical long
sweet-sweating nights, when Jason came down,
like a golden god, she said, upon her. *O how
he thrilled me then,* she said, *and he was good,
too, strong and loving before he went nuts
for that coy young tart: the little bitch
built hipless like a boy, with useless breasts
barely bigger than bumps. O I made sure no power
on earth would sing sunbursts within that womb.*

When she spoke like that, madness, I learned,
was rising to slap her, and I could do nothing
to help her. But whether I left her alone
or not, she'd come tearing hard at me
with curses and fists and, swarming me, swear
she'd never collapse: *I'll never go limp again—
never! I'll rage till my tongue scorches rock,*

she said as veins ticked across her temples
and, swelling, stitched seams down her neck.
Scorpions! she cried: *They're fighting to death,
they're fighting deep in me—their stingers!
My God!* she cried: *This pain won't stop
till I learn how to sing—I don't know how—
I sling chaos, chaos slings me. When I pass
by children at play or asleep I curse them—
they shriek and my curses catch fire, their skin
begins sizzling, I stand there entranced,
I stand near the flames and watching them burn
I watch without shame.*

Then one morning she was gone and never came back,
and no one I know ever discovered where she went,
but even now sometimes during wind-bothered nights
when the moon hangs gibbous and a lone puma screams
near the top of Iron Mesa, memory shouts at me:
I did, I did see her, I'm sure of it, from the side,
last week, studying leeks at market. I passed
by her twice. No, not then, not last week,
I saw her last month, in Veracruz, on the street—
no, not her, not there, but in Zacatecas last year.
I have seen her, though, and I still see her.
Her eyes, like a hawk's talons flexed for snakes,
come at me cold and dun and sharp, crazed
with spleen and grief. *And all those mad wild cats,*
she says, *that wail out there, like tortured ghosts,
that prowl out there where lava lies, are dreams
of mine, and all the children I set on fire are me.*

Eschatology

SANDRA BLYSTONE

Leslie turns forty
on this warm April night
and throws a party on the patio,
candles glowing like campfires
on tables heavy with food.
An evening breeze stirs the cottonwood tree
that nests the great horned owl
who looks down on us
with neon eyes, unblinking.

I float out of my body,
not supernaturally, but with the third eye
that tequila opens.
At one table a guest makes dromedaries
out of candle wax
and circles them round the middle eastern sweets
like a caravan camped for the night.

In the paddocks, the horses
are shadows and ghostlike bulk, more
a felt displacement of air
than the brown sleek sweating creatures
I have seen here in daylight.
They shy sideways as the dark wind
catches my skirt. To them
I am the ghost.

Inside, someone's long pale fingers
pick a moth from the flan
and push open the kitchen door
to free it. The door falls
heavy and definite
out into the night
and the moth flutters back to the party lights.

I float out also, down, down
to the onion field, out here
on the edge of Texas where stars
are 20 karats. A slight
figure from the far farm
opens a sluice and Rio Grande water
floods the furrowed rows.

The stalks look black
against the star-filled water
but with my third eye
they are green as emeralds,
the whole field emeralds on silver.

And here in the onion field,
stars lapping at my feet,
I see, with my third eye,
the fertile earth freefall. Hot membranes
swell and plump and suck it down,
where it fastens,
doubling in size and doubling again
to a steady, heavy beat

that is my own heart taking me forward
pulse by pulse
to forty, to eighty,
to that last moment
when I will mingle with this water,
this dirt, these stars—
with everything
that right at this moment
I can reach out and touch.

Feast of the Epiphany

SANDRA BLYSTONE

I bought a bell
cast in heavy bronze—
a cross cut in the side—
and hung it on a beam
where it moons the desert wind
with fat boos and clangs.
Tonight it sings in sunset,
tossing off Bach
with hollow copper notes.

The distant mountain melts
in a puddle of fire.
As night gels, shadows blown by wind
ricochet off rocks
while the lion that marked
my birth prowls the universe.
The ice-cold stars
stare me down, plating me
with thousand-year-old silver.

Body Identified

LAURA TOHE

That Thursday afternoon when I
was getting dressed for work,
the newspaper landed with a dull thud on the steps.
It must have
kicked up the dust a little.
And as I combed out my hair, my mom
came across the paragraph:
"Young male Indian
in the early 20's found alongside the highway near Twin
Lakes."

My God, it was on a Greyhound bus in Durango
that I first told you I loved you.
The girl who sat behind us must've heard me make such bold
confessions
through the space between the seats.
Then in silence I fell asleep on your lap.
You must've watched me
dream the La Plata Mountains alone.
The words I uttered weren't enough to keep you.
The nights we clung together
rejected us
and now your life had erupted all over the highway.
In April
you came to pick up that black and white sweater from my
closet.

After the services
I remember wanting to swerve off the highway and into the
sagebrush.
You died for me
one June summer day
in one paragraph of the newspaper.

The Wall

JOHN MARTINEZ WESTON

Last summer Albuquerque was selected as one of the cities to host "The Moving Wall," a one-half size replica of the Viet Nam Veterans Memorial in Washington, D.C. Naturally, all my friends who know I am a 'Nam vet expected that I would go to see it, and some invited me to go with them. I finally agreed to go with a friend of mine, a friend who is also a 'Nam vet.

But as the day grew closer I began to vacillate, and finally, the day before we were supposed to go, I found I couldn't. I didn't know why; I just knew I couldn't. Only now, over a year later, do I really understand why.

It was Pinky. Pinky, the guy I've thought of every day for twenty years, the guy whose memory has influenced my life and my thinking more than anything or anyone else, before or since.

It was early '69 when I first saw him. I had already seen six months of combat, and I had already become my mother's worst nightmare. I had become, at eighteen, uncaring and unfeeling. I had seen my friends go home with hideous wounds, and I had seen my friends go home in bags. I had watched the gang-rape of a thirteen-year-old girl, while bored officers and N.C.O.'s played cards twenty feet away; and I had seen my friend blow his own brains out with an M-16. I had seen bodies mutilated for all kinds of reasons, and for no reason at all. I had seen men shoot themselves, and I had seen them shoot each other, and I was sick of it. I had resolved to never get close to another human being, and I was doing a hell of a good job of it, too. Then came Pinky.

I had been out minesweeping for the "Cav," the First Cavalry Division. This particular company was a gung-ho bunch of cowboys, and a week with them was like a year in hell. Their calling-card was a First Cav patch stuck in the area where a dead V.C.'s genitals used to be— used to be before they were cut off and shoved into his mouth. Not ones to discriminate on account of sex, the Cav also afforded equal treatment to women's bodies. Naturally, the V.C. were more than willing to respond in kind, with the end result being everyone in the unit was afraid to wear their own patch, and I was deathly afraid of being caught with them. At the end of my week, I jumped a chopper back to base camp, waving goodbye to the poor fool who was replacing me. I never saw him again; he stepped on a pressure-detonated mine two days later. The biggest piece of him they found was his right foot, still in the boot.

Once back at Tay Ninh base camp, I immediately headed for my hootch, the sad half-hovel, half-bunker that was home for me and the three other minesweepers in my squad. I squeezed through the narrow, sand-bagged doorway and into the small, dark communal room. I felt, rather than saw someone in there with me, and on reflex I hit the switch of the flashlight on the top of my shotgun, at the same time jacking a round of double-aught into the chamber. There in the beam of light sat the blackest black man I had ever seen, his eyes as big as hubcaps and his hands on his chest. "God-damn," he whispered. "God-damn!" It was Pinky.

Once I had established the fact that he was an American, I ignored him, but I sure wondered what the hell he was doing in Parker's area. The answer wasn't long in coming.

"Hi," said a voice behind me, the most melodious, deep bass voice I had ever heard. "I'm Pinky."

I turned around, and with amazed eyes that had finally adjusted to the darkness, I first beheld the man who would save my life.

"Pinky Johnson," he said, and in spite of myself I began to laugh. I hadn't laughed in months, but it felt so good I just couldn't stop. I laughed until I cried; I laughed until I collapsed on my cot; I laughed so hard I almost pissed my pants.

"I'm Parker's replacement," he said, and stuck out a huge hand. Suddenly he smiled, and I swear it was like someone had turned on a streetlamp in an alley. He had the biggest, whitest teeth I'd ever seen, and his smile made me feel good for the first time in months. Again in spite of myself, I stuck out my hand and watched it disappear into his.

"I don't think my name is funny," he said. "Why do you think it's funny?" And then he began to laugh, too. Ten minutes later we were fast friends, and in a few weeks we were inseparable.

Pinky was from Mississippi, some little cotton town where he was as unaccustomed to Chicanos as I was to black people in Kansas. And yet we became closer than family, closer than brothers. I smoked his first joint with him, and we read each other's letters. We pulled interminable hours of guard duty together, and before long he knew more about me than anyone, even my mother. I don't know if it was the constant proximity of death, or the boredom, or what, but whatever it was, we grew to love each other in spite of my certain knowledge that it was better not to care.

And I wasn't the only one. Everyone liked Pinky. Even the officers, who never liked anyone, liked him. He always had a smile, and he never lost the innocence that some mistook for naiveté. In the company of wolves, Pinky was a lamb. In the black hole of war he was a burning candle; in a land of swaggering, posturing boys he was a man. He stood out from the rest of us like a lily in a coal pile, and he never changed.

Finally the day came when I was going home and Pinky was staying. I had said goodbye to everyone else, and I walked into my hootch to pick up my duffle bag and say goodbye to Pinky. He was sitting on his cot with these big, fat tears rolling off his cheeks and a smile on his face.

"I'm gonna miss you, coyote," he said, and then he got up and hugged me, hard. For the first time in twelve months I cried, too, and hugged him back.

"I'm gonna miss you, too, you big, black gorilla," I said. "Take care of your ugly self." And then I grabbed my bag, spun around, and never looked back.

Three months later I was in Washington, D.C., bummed out, mad at the whole world, and still in the Army. I had left Viet Nam, but it hadn't left me. I felt guilty to be alive, and I had made up my mind to go back to Viet Nam, for as much as I hated it, it was the only thing that was real. I didn't fit in "the world" any more, and I didn't fit into my family. The nineteen-year-olds I had graduated with one year earlier were like beings from another planet to me, and even cars seemed stupid.

And then I got a letter from a friend who was still in 'Nam. He told me that he had heard Pinky had been killed, shot off the side of a tank while he was taking pictures of some kids.

I read somewhere that the first reaction when someone is told they have a fatal disease is denial. I guess that's the way it was with me and Pinky. I never wrote to my friend or anyone else to find out for sure if he was dead back then, and I can't go see his name on a wall now. There are other names there that I know, and there are other memories of other young men that I cherish. But Pinky is different.

Pinky saved my life. Not in the usual way, the way you see on TV, not by pulling me away from machine gun fire or throwing himself on a grenade or anything like that. He saved my life by being a man when it was easy to be much less; he saved my life by showing me even the biggest man can be gentle and caring. Were it not for Pinky, I would have died long ago, either in Viet Nam or soon after; if not by my own hand, then surely by someone else's.

But Pinky's memory would not allow that. Whenever times got bad, I remembered a time when they were much worse, and I remembered a smiling, black face with the most incongruous name ever attached to it. I remembered a goodness that would not be bowed and a spirit that never crawled. And I vowed that I would live my life in memory of his. And I have tried.

I think of him every day, not just on Memorial Day. I, too, hurt where the bullets hit him, and I ache for the life he was denied. The people I have loved, I have loved for him, too; and any joy in my life I have shared with him. Pinky's not dead; he lives forever in my heart, forever nineteen.

And so that is why I cannot go to "The Wall." I've already got a wall in my soul that is a mile high and ten miles long, and it bears only one name. And if I ever saw that name on that other wall, I don't know what I'd do. Break down—for sure. Lose my own desire to live—probably. Find peace—doubtfully. All I know for sure is that those are people, not just names.

And I already know enough about walls.

Apartment #4

PENELOPE GILLEN

She was playing with the blade of a Swiss Army knife when she told me that she was considering suicide again. I tried not to look too obvious while I watched her watch me gulp down all the saliva in my mouth. I was in a mild hurry when she came by. A kind of hurry that became an urgency in order to avoid the suicide discussion. I listened just as obediently and patiently as the last time. My main concern was not to hear her but to say "yeah, yeah" at the right intervals and not to ask a lot of personal questions. She cried a little about an ex-boyfriend and a little about a current one. She laughed at her own hope for saying that she wanted to live so she could have more bad days in order to gain experience at getting through them.

When I felt sure about her state I did the typical fat person thing and asked her if an ice cream cone would help her to feel better. She gave me the typical fat person response and said yes. I left her at my apartment to do the post suicide discussion routine: wash her face, blow her nose, call her boyfriend and tell him she loved him, while I went for the ice cream.

I got the ice cream first, before I did a few of my own errands so that it would be softening up by the time I got it home. I took too long. The smell of her blood was the same as mine. She did it the way most men would. She cut both wrists first then her throat.

To the Point

MERCEDES LAWRY

Around the capes of sorrow
move the longboats. Not even
a whisk of sound penetrates
the myth. Far past
the cove, two bathers snake
in the green water, in and out
of shadow fans.

I sit here, tight with my secrets,
tasting the rust in the damp air.
Leaning into the rock, I search
for the lost connectives. Where
does the flesh belong in this vulnerable
plan, where forces push and pull
and so much goes disguised? Not so
these trees, this cold, erratic wind.
Even those bathers, for their time
in the water, might have slipped away.

I know how to be afraid.
paralyzed by the levels
of emptiness. How not to fit.

I also know that out in the mountains,
at night, with thick
blackness all around and the small eyes,
distinctions are clear.
Worthiness, inside the circle,
all the harm and blessing,
sleeping then, as one.

The Photographer

CARMELA DELIA LANZA

The dogs are barking again, and
you are pounding on the window,
yelling out to the night
to tell the trees, the houses
surrounding you to be silent.
The dogs do not listen,
they are crying,
hitting their bodies against the wall;
they hear a thunderstorm that doesn't exist yet.

You are in love.
You hold a razor to your throat every morning,
which is imaginary, of course,
but we hold our breaths like a disease,
and your parents leave messages on the machine
begging for a piece of a word,
but you are too busy.
You unlock and lock doors,
the dogs go in and out,
they are digging a warm grave
through the house.

The headlights hit on the dog
by the hedge.
It is small like a rat and that is what you say,
"Look at that little rat, poor pooch,"
and you carefully drive around it.
I sit there and watch your caution,
your small head shrinks even smaller in the shadows.
An hour later the dog is hit,
a soft pillow squeezes under a tire,
a knife through foam.

It cries like a baby,
and I conjure your eyes from the sound;
pity the person who recognizes a twin in spirit.
I put my head under my pillow and forget your hands
on the wheel.
You carefully turn down the wrong street,
the dog runs away at that point,
he still can at that point.

You are not listening to the hit-and-run story,
you drink your orange juice and talk
about stupidity and slow reflexes.
You know the intimate details,
you are not just a metaphor.

You are yelling at the dogs again,
it is before dawn and a storm
is rolling up over the roof.
Strips of negatives tremble in the bathroom;
in a frame grays are more controllable,
and living faces become dead.
She floats down through you
to talk to the dogs,
while they whine under an electric wind,
while your fists roll under your pillow,
waiting for the next explosion.

The Prediction

ALICIA GASPAR DE ALBA

When the child appeared in the village, naked, bloated, and screaming like a cat in heat, Dionisio Acosta knew that his wife's prayers had been answered. For twelve years, Atizania had made the annual pilgrimage to the Basilica de la Soledad in Oaxaca. Thirty-two kilometers later, her knees like the mashed gizzards of a chicken, Atizania would prostrate herself before the crowned Virgin and pray for the child's arrival. This is not what she told Dionisio she was praying for, but the truth, as always, leaked out, and for twelve years, Dionisio had been using his eyesight with the lust of a doomed bull.

Ciriaco, the deaf-mute curandero of the village, and his mongoloid assistant, Apolonio, came up to where Dionisio was squatting under a fig tree in the plaza, weaving a basket.

"Polo is going to marry that girl," said the mongoloid, pointing to the screaming child who did not look older than two years. Apolonio was twelve.

"Polo has good taste," said Dionisio.

Ciriaco made a series of signs to his assistant and the boy translated. "Ciriaco says that's Atizania's baby."

Dionisio spit a stream of tobacco juice over his shoulder. "I know," he said. Dionisio shaded his eyes and looked in the direction of the well where Atizania, surrounded by Placida and Berta and a couple of hungry dogs, was already washing the girl's body.

Ciriaco tapped Dionisio's shoulder. Dionisio looked up at him and Ciriaco pressed his thumb between Dionisio's eyebrows. Apolonio laughed. Dionisio nodded. He didn't need Ciriaco to tell him that the prediction was nearing its climax.

It was a custom in the village that whenever a couple got married, they had to have the curandero predict an important event in their future. For Dionisio and Atizania the prediction had been that they would not bear children for many years, but that a girl-child would one day appear in the village and come to Atizania. After that, Atizania would grow fertile and Dionisio would go blind.

Dionisio watched Ciriaco and his assistant cross the sun-baked road and approach the women at the well. Ciriaco picked up the child and raised her over his head. He inspected the bottom of her feet and smelled her genitals. He placed her against his chest and felt her bloated, sunburned belly. The child kicked and screamed. (No doubt the girl has worms, thought Dionisio.) Ciriaco inspected the girl's toes, and again the girl cried out. Ciriaco gave the child back to Atizania and spoke to her, his hands moving like wings in the bright light. Apolonio translated. Atizania pressed the girl against her, and the girl rested her head in the crook of Atizania's neck, sucking on the tangerine that Atizania had peeled for her during Ciriaco's examination.

Dionisio turned his attention back to his weaving and decided that this had to be the most beautiful basket he had ever made, probably the last one he would ever see. When Atizania came up to show him the child, Dionisio was tempted to give the girl the evil eye. Maybe if she got sick and died . . . but then, the girl touched his chin, cradling it between her brown, sticky hands, and Dionisio was so ashamed of his selfishness, his eyes watered, and he drew the girl to him to hide his face from Atizania. The girl smelled of tangerine and dust and urine. Her brown hair looked like a bird's nest.

"Can she speak?" said Dionisio to his wife.

"She's sick," said Atizania, rubbing the girl's back in circles.

"Worms?"

"Worse. Ciriaco says she's got sugar in the blood. She may not live too long."

Dionisio held the girl at arm's length and looked into her black eyes. The girl frowned. Her nose and cheeks were peeling, as were her shoulders. "She's been out a long time," said Dionisio. "It's a miracle she didn't dehydrate. She must have a strong guardian angel." He tickled the girl under the arms.

"Stop that!" said Atizania. "Tickling isn't good for children. It makes their heart stop."

"I want to see her smile," said Dionisio. "Have you forgotten the second half of the prediction?"

Atizania couldn't meet her husband's eyes. She stared at the little girl's feet. "See those sores between her toes?" she said. "They won't heal because of all the sugar in her blood. That's one of the signs of the disease."

Dionisio picked up one of the girl's legs to examine the sores on her foot. A stream of urine hit him in the face. Dionisio laughed and set her leg down, wiping the urine off with the back of his hand. The girl frowned as she let out the rest of her water. Dionisio had to lift his basket to keep it out of the puddle. "What a stink!" he said, sniffing. "Has this child been drinking mezcal?"

"That's another sign," said Atizania. She untied the bandana from her head and used it to wipe between the girl's legs. "If her urine smells like wet straw and she's got a bloated belly and sores that won't heal—those are all signs of the disease. What are we going to do, Nicho?"

Dionisio spit the wad of tobacco behind him, stretched the corners of his mouth with two fingers, and stuck his tongue out at the girl. The girl mimicked him. "Nothing's going to happen to her," said Dionisio. "If she's sick, we'll take care of her. If she dies, we'll bury her. But I don't think she's going to die." He rubbed the girl's head. "Did Ciriaco say anything about this mark?"

Atizania leaned close to the girl and saw that her husband was pointing to a faint brown mark in the shape of scorpion pincers curving just below the girl's hairline on her forehead.

"Ay, Virgencita!" said Atizania, crossing herself quickly.

"Wherever this child came from," said Dionisio, reaching up to snap a ripe fig off a low-hanging branch, "she's protected, aren't you, Mercedes?"

"Mercedes?" said Atizania. "I promised the Virgin to call her Soledad."

Dionisio handed the fig to the girl and tickled her under the chin. "Mercedes was my mother's name," he said. "We will call her Soledad Mercedes."

The girl stuck her tongue out at Dionisio and toddled off in the direction of a sleeping pig, suckling the stem of the fig like a nipple.

Dionisio stood up and took Atizania in his arms. "Ciriaco's predictions always come true," he murmured. "But I'm not afraid anymore. A father can't be afraid."

Atizania wept against his shoulder.

Early the next morning, before the priests and the tourists arrived in the pueblo, they baptized Soledad Mercedes in the central patio of the ruins. Ciriaco officiated over the ceremony, wearing necklaces of lapis lazuli, amethyst, and turquoise. Apolonio wore a beaded headband with turkey feathers hanging down the back. Dionisio looked pale and sleepy. He had not closed his eyes all night.

After dinner, he had worked on his basket until his fingertips were so raw, even the wind hurt them. He had blown out his lamp, then, and walked across town to the ruins, wanting to lie down on the sacred stones of Mitla and fill his eyes with the falling stars. He'd spent the rest of the night at La Sorpresa, drinking with Matías and his future compadre, Silverio, who was to be Soledad Mercedes's godfather. Near daybreak, he'd climbed the hill that overlooked Mitla and watched the sunrise polish the four domes of the church. Below and beside the church, the ancient ruins crumbled. Then, Dionisio had trudged home to shave and eat his breakfast.

The three of them wore yellow, as was the custom. Dionisio in a freshly ironed yellow *guayabera* and white pants. Atizania in a yellow *huipíl* embroidered with peacocks. Soledad Mercedes all wrapped up in the yellow *sarape* that was her godparents' baptism gift.

The patio was filled with people. The women had daisies in their hair and the men wore their black shoes. Dionisio imagined that the Mixtec lords and priests had come out of their catacombs to witness the baptism, and he could see them sitting on the steps in front of the palaces in their bright *penachos*.

The ceremony was a simple one. Ciriaco held a burning censor and Apolonio beside him, a bowl of water and a knife, and together they lifted these implements to the sky. Ciriaco mumbled wordlessly. Apolonio called to the Man of the Thunderbolt and the Mother of the Corn to bless the child with strength and fertility. Next, Ciriaco put the censor on the ground and passed Soledad Mercedes over the smoke four times. Apolonio gave the knife to Silverio, who made an incision on his thumb and another one on his wife's thumb, and each of them painted a cross on the girl's forehead with their blood. Ciriaco washed the blood away with the water and passed Soledad Mercedes over the incense smoke four more times. The girl slept through the whole thing.

After the ceremony, they made a procession to Silverio and Berta's house, where the fiesta would take place. By the time they reached the house, Dionisio was floating on mezcal and sleeplessness. He saw everything in a tilted light. The people around him looked like the reflections in the crazy mirrors he had seen at the *feria* in Oaxaca. His own feet had become elongated and were so far down that, for a moment, he thought they'd slipped into the catacombs with the lords and priests. He drank another cup of mezcal and watched Soledad Mercedes playing with the other children. He remembered he had to finish his basket, and sent one of Silverio's sons to fetch it for him.

When the boy came back, Dionisio squatted under a mulberry tree and finished stitching the last scorpion into the basket. Atizania brought him a plate of tamales and rice, and fed him while he worked. The pink and blue pincers of the other scorpions on the basket snapped at his food.

"Be careful," he told Atizania. "These scorpions are alive. Look! Now they're dancing a *jarabe tapatio!*"

Atizania rolled her eyes and shook her head. "You need to sleep," she said.

After he had finished eating, Dionisio called for another bottle of mezcal and asked the *conjunto* to play songs of the revolution. Silverio brought him the mezcal and poured each of them a generous amount in their tin cups.

"Compadre," said Silverio, squatting beside Dionisio. "This is a fiesta. You're not supposed to be working."

"I have to finish this, Compadre," said Dionisio. "No telling when the blindness will strike."

Silverio squinted at Dionisio's basket. "What kind of design is that, Compadre?" he asked.

"You like it?" said Dionisio.

Silverio nodded. "Very original, Compadre. You could probably get 500 pesos for it in Oaxaca, maybe more if you go during the margarita hour."

Dionisio chuckled. "No, Compadre," he said, "this is no turista basket. This is a gift for my little girl. Besides, she's the one who gave me the idea for the design."

"How did she do that, Compadre?"

"By standing in front of me, Compadre. How else?"

Silverio cracked up laughing. "At least you haven't lost your sense of humor, Compadre," he said, holding up his cup. "Here's to a good sense of humor."

"And to Mitla," said Dionisio, hitting his cup against Silverio's.

The two of them were quiet for a moment, Dionisio threading the thin cord of the handles through the bottom of the basket, Silverio listening to "La Adelita." When the song was over, Silverio said:

"Hey, Compadre, do you know what Ciriaco told Matías? He said some big changes are coming to Mitla."

"Is that right, Compadre?" Dionisio said sarcastically.

"Really!" said Silverio. "It's going to affect everybody, not just you, Compadre. It's going to affect all of the Republic. Ciriaco says Mitla is going to sink."

"Ciriaco talks too much," said Dionisio. "Do me a favor, Compadre. Tell me if these two handles are the same length. All this mezcal has twisted my vision."

Silverio tucked one of the handles further into the basket and moved up the knot. "You know what else Ciriaco said?" Silverio whispered. "He said that when you go blind you're going to be a seer."

"Well, Compadre," chuckled Dionisio, "I guess if the mute can talk, the blind can see."

"Salúd!" said Silverio, and they toasted again.

Dionisio spent the rest of the afternoon singing with the group of men that had gathered around the *conjunto*. When Atizania came and took his hand and led him to a hammock on the side of Silverio's house, Dionisio lay down obediently and promised to sleep. But his eyes did not want to close. Through the leaves of the tamarind trees he could see the clouds shifting. He saw a hummingbird and a beehive and spotted a kite stuck in the top branches of the mulberry. Then, he caught a flash of green and blue in the corner of his eye. *The scorpions must be following me*, he laughed to himself, but suddenly a parrot perched on a limb above him and the intensity of the bird's gaze startled Dionisio. He became aware of a deep fear settling in his bones. He had been awake two full days now, swallowing everything he could with his vision, and still the blindness had not come. And now this parrot, which he had never seen in the village before, was looking at him as though to determine his fate. Dionisio reached a hand down and found a pebble and prepared to throw it at the parrot, but a great fatigue came over him and he could not raise his hand. He could not even keep his eyelids open.

When Dionisio awoke from his siesta, Soledad Mercedes was sleeping beside him, her cheek resting in a pool of her own saliva on his shoulder. Above him, he saw the stars through the dark lattice of the branches. Atizania found him weeping.

Five months passed, and still, Dionisio's eyesight had not left him. Ciriaco explained that it would not happen until Atizania was with child, and Dionisio had taken to relieving his need with the women at *La Sorpresa*. Atizania did not bother him about it, understanding that in this way, Dionisio avoided fulfilling Ciriaco's prediction. But one Saturday afternoon, upon returning from the market in Oaxaca, Dionisio saw the parrot again. It was perched on the roof of his hut, its blue-green wings bright as semaphores in the dusty afternoon. The neighbors had gathered in the middle of the road to stare at it, none of them more aware than Dionisio that the parrot was the omen of his blindness. Atizania was waiting for him at the door, her scapular hanging over her blouse.

"Tell them to go away," Atizania whispered as Dionisio came in. "They're scaring me, Nicho."

"Come here," said Dionisio behind her. "Don't you realize what that parrot is?"

"I've never seen it before," said Atizania.

"You've never seen me blind, either," he said, leading her to the back of the hut.

"Nicho, it's not a good idea," she said.

He stripped her slowly, amazed at the different shades of her body, the deep bronze of her arms and legs, the pink-gold of her breasts and buttocks. He took her in his favorite way. When his moment came, he clenched his jaw to keep from waking Soledad Mercedes.

On Monday, while guiding three Canadian ladies through the ruins, Dionisio's sombrero was blown off by the wind. He chased after it, caught it before it tumbled into the churchyard, and pushed it down on his head. A twig had gotten hooked on the brim of the sombrero and was dangling over his forehead. He was just about to pull it off, when he realized that the twig was a scorpion's tail, arching down to sting him between the eyebrows. The last thing Dionisio saw before the sight drained out of his eyes was the crucifix on one of the cupolas of the church.

Manon Welcomes the Return of the Hot Season

MARTHA ELIZABETH

Eyes meeting over the chicken thighs
as the Serengeti animals
race and mate across the plains
on public television, a kiss
on your way to trim the lawn,
licking your lips—
I smell in the distance the hot
underbreath of summer.
The backyard is a savannah, overrun
with wildflowers, herds of color
jostling in the wind, and you
are circling, bringing down
stragglers at the edge.
The surge of motor in the yard
sounds like the roar of a lion.
Do not be surprised
if you do not see me when you return.
Do not be surprised
if you are ambushed
in your own house.

Stars

BRIAN SWANN

The horse drive followed a crow, but
the livestock were driven to the western fringes

of the Colorado desert, to forage by
Agua Hedionda. The men were careful where they

spat. If you drive over a chew of tobacco
the wagon will break down. They carried

rolled barley for the saddle horses.
Four flakes of a bale of hay tided them over

till the Cuyamaca Mountains loomed on the right,
round a turn in the grade. The Tayui well,

five by six, was brackish, but the ground
was damp with a little salt sod grass.

They cut galleta so brittle it sounded
like the horses were chewing sodacrackers.

Dug a post hole for water. The donkey drained one,
then another. Most nights the west wind blows

in the desert. This was one night it didn't.
Stars. Stars. Stars. They turned into

their blankets, but couldn't sleep. They lay
on their backs, eyes open, faces empty, full of stars.

The Other Grandma

TRICIA BAATZ

Until a couple of years ago, when I was nine, me and my brother Ray lived with our Grandma Stacy who was our Ma's mother and lived in this dinky town in Northern Minnesota. I liked her fine because she swore like a trooper and taught me how to read these fancy cards called tarot. She did other stuff I liked, too, made popcorn for dinner and played the Ouija Board with me and embroidered pillow cases that had fine ladies on them who stood around in the flower garden wearing big skirts and holding little frilly umbrellas called parasols.

Ray didn't fare too well up there, though, because he hated small town living. He called the other boys a bunch of dumb farmers so naturally he didn't have any friends but yours truly and the next thing you know he wound up back in Minneapolis in a home for juvenile delinquents because they say he stole some dumb farmer's car. I wrote him a letter that said *Dear Ray, Good going. I bet you're very happy being in the city again, seeing all the sights and getting around town.* I thought this was very funny in a smart-aleck sort of way, but really I missed Ray very much and sometimes thinking about him behind bars eating off a tin plate made me cry at night. I'd get out of bed and switch on the Mary and her Little Lamb lamp and look at this envelope full of photographs I had, picutres of me and Ray and Grandma Stacy. Some of them were taken in Grandma's backyard near the crab apple tree. In one of those I'm faking a scream and bugging my eyes out while Ray holds a hatchet over my head, about to bury it in my skull. He's wearing an evil grin on his face. In another picture we're sitting under the tree, me in Ray's lap, and a grey-striped kitty in my lap Ray gave me who I called Ray Junior. Grandma's standing behind us, smiling, her arms laced into the tree as if they were branches. I had to give the kitty back to another girl after it turned out Ray had stolen him for me.

My favorite picture was taken at the county fair the summer Ray got hauled off to the boys' jail. I'm sitting on a pony at the pony rides and Ray is standing in front of me. He wouldn't sit on a pony because it wasn't a real horse, he said, and besides he was too big. His hand is on the pony's mane, touching my fingers. Ray's got a bandana tied around his neck and a straw cowboy hat stuck on the back of his head. He liked to pretend he was Little Joe on *Bonanza,* and he kind of looked like him, too, with his curly dark hair and handsome smile. Ray used to be kind in a secret sort of way known only to me. I wish now I had told Ray in my letters how much I missed him and all. Maybe then he'd still love me.

After Ray got sent to jail, me and Grandma Stacy figured there were still two bad things to come, as trouble travels in threes. When she laid the cards out on the table at night they were full of swords and lightning bolts, fire and dead men. She'd rub her nose and study them, give me a sly look and push them all together, put them back in the deck. "Hell's bells," she'd say, "aren't you tired of these old cards?" She'd blow out the candles and turn on the lights.

I hate it when old folks don't want you to know what's going on, like when I'd go into town with Grandma and people would walk up and say, "Stacy, this child is the spitting image of her mother." They'd shake their crummy Lutheran heads at her like it was a curse, like I was so dumb I didn't see or hear what was going on. If I asked Grandma Stacy what they meant, she'd tell me they didn't mean anything, or not to worry about it, or she'd say "Let's go into Woolworth's and see if they got any of those Wedding Paper Dolls." When we got home and put the groceries and other stuff away, I'd go take a good look at myself in the hall mirror. Maybe my Ma was real ugly, I thought. I pushed my hair back with my hands, it went everywhere, like a pile of yellow straw. Maybe that was wrong. I leaned into the mirror and looked at my eyes. They were big and blue and loony-looking. My legs were too long, my mouth was crooked, I was a real mess. No wonder no one stuck around me for very long.

Then one day one of the farm boys told me my father was a convict like my brother Ray and my mother was a tramp just like me. "Go piss up a rope," I said, a pea out of the pod of Stacy and Ray. The point of the whole story is that after a while I put two and two together and figured out everyone was telling Stacy I was going to wind up being a tramp like my Ma who I don't even remember hardly because she kept dumping us off at foster homes until we wound up with Grandma Stacy when I was five and Ray was around ten or so. I felt so lousy I sat on the front steps and stared at the sun until it dropped out of sight, too, leaving the clouds all blue and violet.

I wrote Ray a letter every night of my life and told him about *Bonanza* and *Gunsmoke* and *Mighty Mouse.* There was no TV in the delinquent home, and telling these heroic stories to Ray made the letters longer and I hoped they cheered him up. He wrote back once a week, telling me hilarious stories about jail life. Ray had a real talent for turning a bad situation into a joke. One night as I sat at the kitchen table, I read a part of the letter to Grandma Stacy that said the warden at the place looked like Hoss Cartwright's half-wit twin. That just about split my gut. Grandma stood at the stove, scraping potatoes and onions in a skillet and shook her head. "What am I going to do with two children who laugh at crime and punishment?" she asked. Her face looked old and tired and scared me a little.

"If you don't laugh you end up crying all the time," I said. "You don't want a couple cry babies on your hands, do you?"

She was silent and far away. I could hear only the scraping sound in the pan, and it felt like pins in my ears. I hopped off my chair and started to gallop around the kitchen, singing the *Bonanza* theme song. Then I switched to *Here he comes to save the day, it means that Mighty Mouse is on his way!* but nothing made Grandma laugh or even move. I was real scared; there were snakes and frogs that slithered and jumped in my belly. I ran up behind her and yanked her apron string but instead of laughing she turned on me and yelled "Stop it, Loretta!"

She may as well have punched me in the face. I'm not Loretta. Loretta was my mother the tramp who ran off with the unknown convict who screwed up my brother's genes. Everyone knows my name is Carrie. *Crazy Carrie, Crazy Carrie, Crazy Carrie.*

I thought I was in for another move. I made myself be quiet and set the table for supper, tried hard to be a good kid even though it's completely against my nature. When Grandma sat down she pulled me on her lap and told me "Don't pay any attention to me. I'm just worried and sorry." She squeezed me and put angel kisses on my head. After supper we cleared off the table and put the dirty dishes in a wash pan in the oven, so in case anyone stopped by they wouldn't think we were lazy. I put a little square luncheon cloth on the table and lit the candles. "I'll read *your* cards tonight," I told her. She put her hand on her throat and the corners of her mouth twisted up in a funny smile. "Sometimes it's good to read, sometimes not," she said, but I said, "Oh, Gram, it's just a game." I shuffled the cards and had her cut them twice with her left hand, and when I turned them over one by one on the table swords of worry and pain were everywhere and the Tower on fire being struck by lightning stood straight up in front of me, about to tumble down. "Looks like we're in for some trouble here," I said, "so we better hang on for a rough ride."

I was finished with the cards so we watched some television. *The*

Alfred Hitchcock Show was about a lady who hit and killed her husband with a frozen leg of lamb and then cooked it up and served it to the cops who couldn't figure out what the murder weapon was. It was about the funniest thing I ever saw, so I began to write about it to Ray, but thought Warden Hoss might get his hands on it and think it was a conspiracy or something.

When it was time to go to bed I felt kind of scared again, all of a sudden and for no reason, but Grandma said it was fine if I slept with her and that she could use the company. We huddled together in bed and Grandma told me about some fairies in the woods in the middle of summer dream. I traced my finger over the ladies on the pillow cases, then I floated way up into The Sun and the next thing I knew it was morning.

The day was hot and green so we sat in the shady parts, mostly, near the house and made dolls out of hollyhocks. The way to do this is to turn an open flower upside down and shove a toothpick through it, then stick a bud on top for the head. Grandma showed me how to do this, and how to roll the toothpick between my thumb and finger to make them dance. They had big pink skirts with little green capes on them that twirled and twirled. I made Grandma dance with me, too, and she spun me around until my feet left the earth and I would have flown away into space except that she held tight to my hands. She had to slow down and stop, she was laughing so hard and was out of breath. She said "I'm going to croak if I don't stop laughing," and she went and got a bowl and her sun hat and went into the garden to pick some peas.

I pulled up a fistful of grass and laid it on the steps to make a bed for my dolls. I pulled two big leaves from the maple tree and used them as blankets to cover them up.

I hollered for Grandma to come see but when I turned and looked at her she was lying in the garden, her hat knocked off, the bowl turned over on its side.

When you look into the face of someone you love who's dead, a thousand thoughts rush into your brain all at once. I wondered if Grandma was cold, if she knew she was dead, if I could ever eat peas again, where was I going to sleep that night, who I should tell, where was I, I wanted my brother Ray, did she really laugh herself to death, or did I kill her, spinning into the sky?

Someone screamed her head off right near me, she screamed and screamed and I wanted her to stop, but there was no one in the world there but me, so I made my hand go up over my mouth to stop it but it didn't stop.

The next thing I remember there was a funeral in a place called a funeral *home* which didn't make any sense because nobody really lives there, do they? A lot of people who knew Grandma Stacy came to the funeral, whether they were her friends or not, and I kept my eyes and ears open thinking just maybe my mother would show up and I could see if I really looked like her or not, but instead I heard one of those rotten farm boys mutter "That crazy nigger's back," and I turned my head and there was my brother Ray in a blue suit that fell off his shoulders, his hair chopped short, with some fat guy I didn't know with his hand on Ray's shoulder. I ran to him as he stepped up to the coffin, which bothered me because it hung wide open. His shoulders were up too high so I put my hand on his back, and when he saw me he bent over and hugged me and began to bawl like a baby. This shocked me to no end because I had never once before or since seen Ray shed a single tear.

He picked me up right off the ground and put his face close to mine and said "How you doing?" and I said "Fine." Then I looked at his shiny black eyes and his honey-colored skin and said "Ray, I never knew before that we were colored." He caught a little laugh in his throat and smiled at me but right when he was going to tell me something some old lady with a wrinkled hanky came up and whispered "You children put your grandmother in her grave." The flowers in the place smelled like dead things and I almost threw up.

Ray had to go back the same night. I stayed at the neighbor ladies' house called the Hess sisters who were fat and warm and nice, they wore rouge and lipstick all the time and let me put it on in the house only, they made a big deal over me and called me "poor baby," but it was okay, I got along okay. They took me to see a movie show called *Lilies of the Field* that had a bunch of nuns in it and this very handsome man named Sidney Poitier. The more I watched him the more it seemed to me he looked like Ray, only darker. I figured maybe Sidney Poitier was our real father, not the convict. We never got to see him because he was far away in Hollywood making movies and stuff all the time. He was very nice, he smiled just like Ray. That night I wrote Ray a letter about the movie but I didn't tell him Sidney Poitier was our father.

When I fell asleep I dreamt I stood on top of the Tower with Grandma Stacy and Ray. We laughed and spun around holding hands. My flower dolls fell over the edge and when I reached for them I fell, too, and Grandma and Ray held their arms out to me, but they couldn't stop me from falling.

After a few days the Hess sisters said they had a surprise for me.

They told me I was going to live with my grandma. I didn't understand. I thought they had gone off the deep end.

"My grandma's dead," I told them.

"The other grandma," they said, all smiles and thrills.

"Well, fine," I said, "I don't like you, either." I stomped off into the next room and stopped dead in my tracks. An old lady with beauty parlor hair stood there wearing a suit in the middle of summer. Her hands flew up to her face at the sight of me, she cried "Oh, Caroline!" and dropped to her knees like she just saw the Holy Ghost. She held out her arms wide as a bear trap and looked so phony I hated her on the spot.

Since I have no say about what I do and where I get to do it, I had to go live with the other grandma in St. Paul. She only let me take my envelope of pictures and a couple of sets of pillow cases. I tried to take the tarot cards, too, but she said "What's in the little silk bag, dear?" and when I showed her she almost keeled over and flung them into the trash, and made the sign of the cross about a million times like a lunatic.

I wrote long letters to Ray who was now just across the river from me and told him all about how the other grandma put me in a Catholic school where I had to wear a white uniform blouse and an ugly red and green plaid uniform skirt that scratched my legs all the time. I told him how we had to pray when we woke up, before we went to sleep and every time we sat down to eat. And how one time, when I said *hell's bells*, she made me hold out my arm and smacked me on the fingers with a wooden spoon, and that hurt like hell.

Two things I liked at the other grandma's house were her porch swing and this guy named Ralph. September nights I would lie on the porch swing and the other grandma would sit in her white wicker rocker and listen to the baseball game on WCCO radio. Once in a while she would stare off through the screens and pull her sweater around her shoulders, stare off into the darkness and say, "Peter and I used to go to the baseball games together, the Minneapolis Millers back then. We'd go on the streetcar, it only cost a dime." Peter was dead a long time already. I guess he would have been our other grandpa. He built this whole house for her, even the porch swing I was rocking in. She'd sigh and look at her lumpy old hands and I felt pretty sorry for her. It almost made me love her, but not like Stacy and not like Ray. I don't think you can help who you love. I really don't.

Also, I liked Ralph who was this crazy guy who did work around the house, like the garden and lawn and plastering cracks. He called me his little helper and let me hang around with him in the garage.

He drank from a bottle that had a brown paper lunch sack wrapped around it. He was old with black and white whiskers sticking out of his face, but when he drank out of the lunch sack he acted like a kid, he danced around with me and did his Popeye imitation and showed me a tattoo on his arm of a mermaid with bare boobs that got bigger when he flexed his muscle. Then he'd start in telling me these jokes that he thought were very funny, but I didn't usually get them. He always had lots of sticks of Wrigley's spearmint gum that he'd share with me so the "old girl won't be none the wiser," as he would say.

One day I complained to Ralph about how me and the other grandma really drove each other over the edge with the way we both ate, about how I used my fingers and the back of my sleeve and she was very particular about forks and knives and napkins. And of saying grace, of course. You could be starving to death but still had to pray first.

"She's just trying to do the best for ya, Carrie," he said. "She likes to look out after all us heathens." He took a swig out of his sack. "Don't be so rough on the old girl. You're all she's got left, you know." He drank some more, he laughed. "The Virgin Mother and the little heathen," he laughed harder and poked me with his elbow, hanging on to his sack for all he was worth. "Why do the heathens rage?" he asked and leaned against the wall and began to laugh his butt off. Ralph started getting on my nerves, so I left.

On that particular day the other grandma saw me coming out of the garage. She called to me from her bedroom window upstairs and when I got up there was was putting clean white sheets on her bed. She said she wanted to talk to me so I stood at the end of the bed and looked at her, but she wouldn't look at me. She said, "What were you doing in the garage so long?"

"I was just playing with Ralph," I said.

"And what was so amusing? I could hear you two laughing way up here."

"I don't know," I said, trying to remember. It was hard to think, the other grandma made me so nervous. I looked at the picture of Saint Theresa that hung over her bed.

"I don't want you spending your time with Ralph," she said. "If you want to do chores there are plenty of things in this house to do more suited to a young lady."

"Is Ralph a heathen?" I asked her. She snorted, her way of laughing. "He certainly is," she said.

"Am I a heathen, too?"

She turned around and narrowed her eyes at me. "Is that what he told you? Why would he say such a thing? What's going on?" Her face was all red and a little of her spit hit me in my face when she said this: "No granddaughter of mine is a heathen! You're a Schroeder!"

"No, I'm not, I'm an O'Toole. Your name is Schroeder." She slapped me a good one across the face and said I could just sit there in that room alone with no supper until I learned to appreciate all the good things God had blessed me with. I sat on the bed then stood in the middle of it and bounced up and down when she shut the door. The face of Saint Theresa kept passing me as I bounced by. She had on a brown nun's outfit and she was holding a cross that had pink and yellow roses falling off of it. Her eyes were screwed up towards heaven. "What's a heathen, anyway?" I asked her, bouncing on my butt and right off the bed.

I looked through the other grandma's dresser drawers but didn't find anything interesting, except an envelope like mine with photographs in it.

One of them was taken in her backyard when she was a young woman in a flowered dress, laughing it up with a guy in a suit who was holding a little boy. It looks like the picture was taken in the springtime. Another picture, the studio kind, was of a young man in an army uniform. On the back it said *Sgt. Michael Paul Schroeder, 1950*. He felt familiar in an odd way, down in the pit of my stomach. He had light hair and eyes and a crooked mouth like me. I put the pictures back in the envelope under her pink corset and shut the dresser drawer fast. After that I wasn't so quick to look into drawers and closets. You never know what you might find. You might be sorry.

I came from school one fall afternoon and got a letter from Ray that said he was getting out. I went crazy, I was so happy. I ran and told the other grandma that Ray was coming home, I couldn't stop screaming and laughing and dancing around the living room. She looked like a brick sitting there, a brick in the Tower. Her arms grew out of the brick like long snarly vines wrapping around me, strangling me.

"Ray cannot come *here*," she said, her face all red, her eyes blinking.

"What do you mean?" I asked. The snakes and frogs woke up in my stomach, doing a crazy dance.

"He's no relation to me, dear," she said, trying to smile at me, but her smile was the smile of the devil.

"Of course he is, you're our other grandma."

"I'm *your* grandma, *your* daddy's mama," she told me, not letting go of me, her face turning all different colors.

"Ray's father was a, was a negro, darling. Don't you understand that?" Her teeth were all white and even like sugar cubes.

"Ray's my brother," I said, but she was so stupid she marched me in front of hall mirror and stuck her head on my shoulder and said "Look! You're a white girl, a pretty little white girl. Ray is only your half-brother, don't you understand?"

All I saw in that mirror was a sorry-looking kid in blonde braids and a white uniform blouse, a kid that sort of looked like the other grandma.

Something happened. Something happened that made hell burst wide open and made all the snakes and frogs leap out and fly into the sky. It scared me to death, I started to scream and holler and cry my eyes out, right in front of the other grandma. I started to yell crazy things at her, my mouth moving way ahead of my brain. "You tramp, you convict, you dumb farmer!" I yelled. The walls were rushing at me, the ceiling falling down. "The tower's falling," I shouted. I felt my uniform blouse choke me so I tore it open. I yelled that the snakes and frogs were going to eat her head off and kill her.

"Half a brother, half a brother," I kept crying and sobbing to beat the band. It made me think of Ray being torn in two. All of a sudden I peed on the carpet, getting my socks and shoes all wet, but I was too far gone to care.

"I want my brother," I said, my voice real hoarse and low, "I want my whole brother."

After that the other grandma had a long talk with a priest named Father Henry who was a very nice guy. They drank coffee and he ate two pieces of chocolate cake and smiled at me a lot and asked how was I doing in school and all. His face was very pink and smooth and hung over his stiff black and white collar. He was what I imagined God would look like, only in a different outfit. He said he beseeched her to open her heart and give Ray the opportunities she had given me. He said it would give her Grace which is something we're supposed to need to get to heaven. I was coloring pictures on the coffee table with crayons and construction paper, but all the while I was listening very closely. I could see he was doing a good job on the other grandma. When he left I gave him a picture I drew of him in a cloud with angel wings. He smiled and his face got pinker. Grandma said Ray could come and stay.

Things just didn't get off to a good start. I sat by the living room window all morning the day Ray was to come, just waiting to run out and grab him, hug him hard, but when he came into the front porch I couldn't move. He looked like a dream through the lace curtains, standing there just staring at the front door. In his right hand he held a little suitcase that looked like doll clothes should be in it. He raised his other hand to knock on the door, but stopped and wiped the sweat off his palm on his jacket and rang the doorbell.

The other grandma opened the door, she just looked at him and said "come in." Ray just stood there. Then she said "Well, young man, are you going to stand there all day?" Ray stuffed his hand in his pocket and walked past her, he saw me and said "Hey, Carrie," in a very soft voice. He really hung on to that little suitcase. I thought my heart would explode. "Oh, Ray, oh, Ray," I said over and over like a broken record. I put my arms around him and pushed my face into his belly. He patted me on my back a little. I wish I had opened the door myself, right away, but it's too late now.

Ray never could think of much to say to the other grandma, and I had forgotten about how he had a habit of breaking things when he was nervous. And maybe he took things, I don't know.

He took things.

The other grandma said, "I don't need this trouble in my life. You're setting a bad example for Caroline. Do you want to go back to Shadderton?"

Ray wouldn't say boo to her if it was Halloween. He'd shrug his shoulders or stare out the windows. One night he lay on the middle of the living room floor, just staring up at the ceiling, and when she started in on him he started rocking back and forth, singing *You ain't nothing but a hound dog, crying all the time*, in a real corny way, but when she got to the *Shadderton* part he pulled himself under the sofa so that his hands and face were hidden under its skirt. "Shadow town, shadow town," he began to sing, in a voice like laughter and crying.

"Stop it, stop it, stop it!" the other grandma yelled, but the more she yelled the louder he sang, until she marched over to where his legs were hanging out from under the sofa and booted him with her big black shoe. But Ray kept singing, and she kept yelling and kicking him with her big stupid foot, until I couldn't stand it and got mixed up and kicked Ray's leg with my tennis shoe. He shot out from under the couch and sprang to his feet. "That hurt," he hollered into my face. He stomped over to the stairs and looked over his shoulder at me. "That really hurt," he said, and went up the stairs.

Later when we were alone together he said "I hate that old biddy! I want to kill her! We could pack up some stuff and get the hell out of here."

I dreamt about the Devil that night. About eternal flames, burning forever. Ray wasn't there to save me. I hollered out for him in the darkness.

"It's okay, Carrie, it's okay," Ray said. He rubbed my back and I woke up. He was sitting on the edge of my bed, smiling at me. "You were having a bad one," he said.

"Why didn't you come and save me?" I cried.

"I'm going to save you, don't worry. We're going to get the hell out of this place, Carrie. Don't worry. Leave it to me." He went over and shut my bedroom door. He said "SHHH!" and hunched his back and made big tip-toe motions toward me. I began to laugh. He got down on his hands and knees and began to sniff around and whine like a dog. He sniffed at my mattress and slid his hands under it. I couldn't believe the loot he had stashed under my bed—some silverware and a gold cross, a little carved-out tray and some money, too. He winked at me and put it all back very carefully. There were frogs in my belly. There were a million snakes.

Ray hopped on my bed and held me in his lap and began to rock me. He began to sing "The White Cliffs of Dover" the way Grandma Stacy used to.

In the morning I woke up and Ray was asleep at the end of my bed, all curled up in a ball. I felt bad because Ray is so tall and he was scrunched up asleep with no blanket. I put my covers over him and put my arms around him. He sort of woke up and put his arm around me, too. Pretty soon after that the other grandma came in and she had a holy fit. "Dear God in Heaven! What's going on here? What are you doing, you filthy little beast?" she screamed. She tried to haul Ray off into another room, but when she grabbed the back of his undershirt he spun around and punched her in the face. She keeled over on the bed, spitting teeth and blood. She made a funny moaning sound like a scared dog.

"Oh, damn, *damn*," Ray said. His arms hung down at his sides, but he danced back and forth on his feet like a boxer. "Man, I'm in big trouble now," he said.

"Carrie!" the other grandma cried, holding one hand out to me. She held her mouth with her other bloody hand. Her glasses were all bent and broken.

I shook all over, standing between Ray and the other grandma. I started to reach out my hand to touch her cold bony fingers, but she screamed "Call the police! Call the police! Tell them to come and take this . . . this. . . ."

"Nigger!" Ray shouted. He stopped dancing on his toes. He turned curtly and walked out to the phone in the hallway near the mirror. He dialed the "0" watching his reflection. "Hello, Operator? Give me the police," he said. He waited. "Yeah, it's an emergency."

"Stop it, Ray," I shouted, running toward him. He held up his hand to stop me. The world was full of hands that said *come here, go away*.

"Yeah, hello," he said, "Better come to 2020 Boniface. There's some crazy nigger here beating on a helpless old white lady." He hung up the phone, still looking at himself in the mirror. He tilted his head down, then raised his eyebrows and stared at himself, touching two fingers to his mouth, then pulling them away as he blew pretend smoke out of the little *o* he made with his lips. Here the cops were coming, and the other grandma was screaming like a banshee, and Ray was doing his Marlon Brando impersonation. He popped his eyes and made a silly grin, saying "That's all folks!" like Porky Pig. He turned his back on the mirror, slid down to the floor, pulled up his knees and began to beat on them like drums, making a *baabaabop* sound and just staring off into space.

"Are you crazy, Ray? Why did you do that?" I hollered at him. I tried to pull him up by his shoulders, but he wouldn't budge.

"Carrie, come here," the other grandma was bawling like a kid. I looked at her over my shoulder, but she was far, far away from my heart.

"Ray, you got to snap out of it," I said. "We have to get out of here now, right away." I thought I heard sirens in the distance, but it wasn't them yet. "Ray, get up!"

All of a sudden Ray came back to earth. He jumped to his feet and started looking all around him like he just woke up from a bad dream. "Carrie," he said, grabbing my shoulders. "I gotta go. I got to run and hide. I'll see about you later. I'll come back later, promise."

"No, Ray, let me come now." I wrapped my arms around him tight, I wouldn't let him go. The other grandma was yelling and yelling my name. It was making thunder and lightning crack and rumble in my head.

"Damn it, Carrie, let go," Ray hollered. "I can't take you with me now. I got to run fast. You can't run fast."

I was sobbing and begging him to take me. He practically broke my fingers off, he was so anxious to get rid of me. He kept shoving me away from him, shoving me back to the other grandma. He ran down the stairs and I followed him. The other grandma screamed "Carrie, Carrie!" in a high, screechy voice that made me scream back. Ray ran out the door, still in his underwear. It was raining out.

I took off after him, but Ray was way ahead of me already. I ran as fast as I could, but I was barefoot and my big toe turned under me and it hurt like crazy. I had on these stupid yellow pajamas with happy bunnies and bears riding bicycles all over them. They were getting all wet, and I started to yank on them. I hated those bunnies and bears with their dumb, grinning faces. It was more than I could stand, and I can stand a lot. I sat down in the middle of the sidewalk.

When I was soaked to the bone a policeman picked me up and carried me into the house. I tried to tell him I beat up on the other grandma but he didn't believe me. There was another one there and they looked at each other and sort of laughed.

The other grandma would never tell me what happened to Ray or where he was. She's one of those people you can't ask too many times. I began to hide in the shadows of the house and listened to her on the phone or when people came by to see her. Pretty soon I put it together that Ray was in a place like Shadderton, only maybe it was worse.

I still have bad dreams at night, but they're different. Mostly I have a dream about the hall mirror. It's like the magic looking glass in the movie *Snow White*, except sometimes when I look in it I see Ray staring back. Other times I look in it and there's the other grandma. I try to run away from her but my feet are like rocks and I can't.

Last Wednesday on my birthday Ralph gave me a baseball and a glove. He played catch with me on the front sidewalk and the other grandma spied on us from the front porch. She said it was a dumb present for a girl. I said it was not and she said yes it was dumb and just like Ralph. I thought about how hard that baseball was and how I liked the way it sort of stung when I caught it in my glove. Later the baseball hit the hall mirror and it smashed into a million pieces. It made a loud noise like all the kids laughing on the playground at once. It was not an accident.

On the next day, Thursday, I got a letter from Ray. He told me what I was afraid of, that he is in a place where crazy people have to stay. He told me Happy Birthday but the rest of the letter made me feel so sad. Except at the very end. He said *Carrie, you have to laugh at the world.*

I think that's a good sign. I think that was a good thing to say.

Compression:
An Essay in Stanzas

DAVID E. HAILEY, JR.

There they are, see them? Four boys riding their bicycles along a trail atop a cliff. See them now? Ages eight, nine, ten, and eleven. It's not a high cliff, only thirty feet or so above a recently mown pasture. The grass, now hay, is piled in the old tradition, in haystacks—one within ten feet of the base of the cliff. The boys stop riding their bicycles and look at that stack below them. Listen, "I'll bet I could ride my bike right into that haystack." "Aw baloney." "Nah, I'll bet." (Here's what it feels like—the Cold. Somebody has shoved my hands in the snow. Wrapped them around iron bars and held them in the snow until they were numb. Wired them through the joints to the iron bar and held them in the wet snow. Wired them through the joints, through the cartilage, wired from joint to joint, icy wire threaded from joint to joint, connecting my fingers each to the other. If I try to open my fist,) *"Hah, do it!"* (little happens, they are really just rigid with cold, but it feels like the wires in my joints prevent them from moving. If I could remove my hands from the bar I could warm them up, but I can't move them {well that's not true, I elect not to stop}— not now. The wires are hollow and filled with liquid nitrogen which leaks through jagged cracks into my joints and into the marrow of my bones. Ice piles up on my gloves, and on my sleeves.

These frigid hands remind me of the brittle fingers of the French soldier left behind in old Russia after Napolean's retreat. Now dead, he lies locked in ice and blowing snow. The blackened fingers grasp at the winter sky, clinging to some invisible object as if trying to pull the man back out of the numbness of his extinction. This seems an exaggeration, but these are real thoughts and sensations.

I pass through Pueblo in the dark. Occasionally, I see a few blurred lights, but mostly I see only the bright reflection of the snow, stars rushing into my headlights. *Why am I here?* Only a madman would ride cross-country in weather like this. Still, I push on, hoping to ride out of this storm before it traps me here where nobody knows me, or likes me. So far the snow is blowing dryly across the road, not sticking.

If it begins to stick, even a little, I'll have to stop. Crank up the speed seventy-two—seventy-three—seventy-four. . . .)

(. . . 102, 103, 104°—the heat in this Utah desert. Sweat glues my hair to the inside of my helmet. But it doesn't cool, no air can get to it. My arms, on the other hand, are bone dry, and burned red by the sun and wind. If I am sweating, it's drying faster than I produce it. My shadow hides under me on the pavement within the shadow of my bike. There's a rest area ahead. It would be nice to pull off, lie in the park in the grass in the shadow of a tree. I consider the question. It would feel good. I watch the turn-off approach and pass without acting. Sweat glues my hair to the inside of my helmet. "Only mad dogs and Englishmen go out in the noonday sun.")

("The hay was stacked in the old style, on a flood plain along a river, under a [seemed like a hundred foot] cliff. The challenge was to ride our bicycles off the bluff into the haystack. I'm the one who made the dare, so I went first.") *I began peddling up the trail, up a short hill away from the edge* (. . . eighty-five miles per hour. That's what the speedometer says. But that's because it doesn't go any higher. The tach says 9,500 RPM—mathematically, that works out to 140 miles per hour. There is a road called "the shotgun," and sometimes "the rifle barrel," a narrow road built in a straight line for forty-five miles.) *of the cliff.* (. . . I stand flat-footed, on this flat road, my helmet off, looking almost the full forty-five miles to the other end. The breeze is gentle, and cool. It lifts my hair out of place and flows gently around the immovable bulk of my body, creating invisible vortices that move off the road and into the desert. Ahead there is nothing but the road. The sun is to my left, not more than half an hour from setting, my shadow extends to my right, like a wing, onto the desert. I watch my shadow pull its helmet on, rev its bike a couple of times, then I turn my attention to the road.) *I turn around and look back down the trail. I can't see the haystack but I know where it is.* (At twenty the breeze is unstable, but at thirty, it's coming steadily from in front—at sixty the wind noise is approximately equal to that of the motorcycle, but it's a buffeting noise, really unpleasant—at seventy-five the wind is the predominant noise and has become laminar—at a hundred it sounds like a huge waterfall—at a hundred and forty it sounds like live steam escaping a pipe. It feels like fast moving water and pushes my faceplate hard against my face. I duck into the space behind my tiny windshield, so the flow skims across the top of my helmet. In here, the predominant sound is the howl of my engine.)

(. . . at two in the morning on a small, bright red racing bike. It's one of those old, corner stations. The kind that used to provide service, but now cuts your belts and punctures your tires when you're not looking.) *"Com'on asshole, quit lookin' an' do somethin'* (A full tank, $3.50, pay cash.—back to use the urinal—it's inside, in the back—then the attendant is gone—a look at a map made of enameled steel, hanging on the wall—25 miles to Denver. The man comes out of the ladies room [strange, why do you suppose he was in the ladies room] he has his arms crossed but I can see the hammer and chamber of a revolver—stainless steel. "Ya' all done?"
"Huh?"
"Got your gas?"
"Yes."
"Had your piss?"
"Well, yes,"—confusion.
"Well, you've had your look at the map," slides the gun out a little more so I can see it better—he needn't have bothered. "Now git your ass on that riceburner and git the fuck outta' here!")

(. . . so fast across the desert. My shadow, my outrigger is flying on the blur of brush, seemingly a foot above the ground. I feel ahead, with all my senses, at this speed just a rock, a board, maybe a chuckhole, a logging truck. The first sign of trouble is a pall of black smoke that emits from both of its stacks. Just a puff, the kind that comes as the driver revs to push a badly tuned diesel into gear. Then a steady stream of black as he begins to accelerate onto the road. By the time he realizes how fast I am coming, I've moved into the left lane and roared past. By the time he's on the road, he's a spot in my rear view mirrors.)

("See if you can lift your foot."
Here's what it feels like. Someone has driven a nail into my knee, through the patella. How can I lift my leg. "The surgery went well," he says. I think he's the one who drove the nail in my knee. "Lift your leg." I look down at my toes. Toes I can barely see beyond the yards of bandage wrapped around my leg. I try to lift my leg. There, I can feel the nail a whole lot better now. There was this uneven floor in my studio. Stepping back to get a better view of a painting. . . .
. . . able to bend my knee enough to ride my motorcycle. There's gravel in the intersection. The bike tries to swap ends with no warning and I'm down, the tank crushes my knee against the asphalt. The shock is short-lived. The pain lasts longer. But I get up, pick up the bike,

mount, and within forty-five minutes I'm cranking through the Alder Lake Canyon, under Mount Rainier.)

(. . . in the lane next to a herd of stampeding cattle. From a distance they looked like ghosts in the rain. Then they looked like a crowd of running people. But then I caught up. How could a herd of cows get on the freeway in the rain? Anyway it's a good thing they are stampeding with the flow of traffic. Getting through them is tricky, a little like driving in sleet and rain in Denver traffic. We can't see, but the cows [in Denver the drivers], in their hurry, don't slow down.)

(A car in a greater hurry, comes up from behind at high speed, and doesn't bother to change lanes before passing. My helmet is filled with my angry curses.)

("I'm bored."
"Boredom is a self-inflicted curse."
"That's stupid."
"Maybe."
She was a sophomore and didn't know where she wanted to major, although she thought she might want to act. Until she decided, she waited tables and drank coffee and complained of boredom.
"It's all in how you look at your life," he said. "You're in an adventure. Why don't you enjoy it?"
She just looked at him. She didn't understand.
"Describe an adventure to me. What makes *The African Queen* such an adventure." (They'd just left the movie *The African Queen*.)
She thought for a while, but her blank, bored look never left.
"They face death," he said. "They become immersed in discomfort, and they face death. We sat in a comfortable, air-conditioned theater and missed half the movie. If the theater had been heated to ninety-five and if the humidity had been ninety-nine, and if they'd released a few thousand tsetse flies and mosquitoes, and if every once in a while an usher had shot one of the moviegoers, then we would have really understood the movie."
"That's stupid."
"Stupid. Let me tell you a real adventure. You are going to spend your life facing obstacles, overcoming some, succumbing to others. One day you will realize you are going to die soon. You'll realize the adventure has been progressing right along without you. Death is right here, right now: disguised as a friend in a booth, or driving towards us from "Cheers," or growing fat and ugly in your brain. Whether you

want to or not, you will live your adventure to the very end—and then you will die—after that you will do nothing but stare at the insides of your coffin and have plenty of time to be bored. If you're bored now, it's because you don't understand the nature of your adventure."

"You're crazy."

"That's true, but I'm not bored.") *"I plummeted through space, the haystack rising towards me. Too late I realized the stack was piled around a pole—that's when I knew I was going to die."*

(I am riding west across the Great Salt desert—as fast as I can go. I see the horizon coming towards me. Always the same horizon. Behind me, time seems to sink away. The sun is just setting. It's a dull red globe, a huge disk spanning the horizon, the sky burns with its light. I push my speed up towards a hundred, thinking to delay the final setting. But in seven minutes the sun is gone. The sky begins to dull. I have no more speed. The sky continues to dull. As I watch the lines in the road flash under me I suddenly realize I'm going backwards. While I'm going forward at 100 miles an hour, the road I'm on is going the other way at 1000 miles an hour. I'm really going backwards at 900 miles an hour. The earth, the solar system, the whole universe rushes at fantastic speeds towards an ultimate entropy. For a second, I suffer vertigo. It's like I'm in an unnoticeable current that's sucking me into a vortex. I can't go fast enough to avoid it. I can't even go fast enough to delay it.)

(New Mexico is an enchanted place. South out of Raton, then west towards Clayton—fast. The road is so recently rebuilt it isn't striped yet. It's just black. So black it's barely visible in my headlights. After a while I pull over, walk out onto the desert. There is no moon, but the stars are so bright, I can see to walk in their light. I walk for what seems like an eternity, looking at the stars, and watching the movement of the sand. After a while I lie down and stare at the stars.)

Listening to Bill Drinkard

THOMAS ALAN HOLMES

I am whitest on the days
I am alone.
Most people do not see me
unless I am with my family—
my mocha wife and ginger daughter.
Then, I am seen, but not very white;
I am suspect. The whispers say,
"Is he colored? Is he passing?
He really could pass."
Curious, questioning whispers wash over my child.

Or I am whitest when I am with my family
and singled out.
Some people see my not-color
contrasting with my family—
my nigger wife and nigger daughter
cause no one to whisper. Hard words,
hard stares sweep over my child.

With that dark arm circling my waist
and that yellow hand grasping my forefinger,
I have the complexion of my parents,
but I am a father, husband, and man.

Ma

MICHAEL ARVEY

for my father, interpreter at Guam War Crime trials,
1949–50. Ma: Space, with a pause; proper timing

1

In the ashen courtroom
your body and hair are my age,
gaunt and a bit gray.

Outside, banyan and papaya trees
stoop from a monsoon. Like a master
wordsmith rebuilding a house
of ruined words,
                you must
peg each nuance
perfectly to the next—

every kanji character
you ever dowelled into memory
tested by the judges of war.

For once
I do not envy your art.

Nor the Guamanians
beheaded for smiling
when B-17's flew over
for Tokyo, or those caught hoarding
skinks and cannibalized for wanting food.

Testimony makes you gag as if
bones were burred in your throat.
Yet somehow you translate.

Clear and precise,
your skill the sole, neutral zone
for the captured soldiers in that room.

2

Years later as a guest
in Japanese homes,
you were honored.

One who'd nod his head
at fine grains
rivered in new wooden floors.
Politely forget words
you no longer wanted to know.

Tractors

JEANNE E. CLARK

Ronnie's the shortest guard in the State of Ohio
Where he is champion
And best kisser of Susan Ellen Haubner. I know.
She says my brother Ronnie kisses like he plays
Basketball, quick and hard. She says he palms her ass
One-handed. Her tits
Two basketballs. She says Ronnie moves
Between her legs as if the whole State of Indiana and its Governor
Came out to see how the game is played.
Ronnie goes with a girl who can talk like that.

Ronnie calls me Einstein. I say
Umbilicus for belly-button.
Bowel movement for   you know. Ronnie says
You can't make Einstein say shit.
On the way to the game Saturday night,
The family rides in a Bel-Air station wagon,
Ronnie rides with the team. In the back of the car,
I read Webster's Dictionary, find
One strong word for each letter in the rival team's name:

Bungarum, venomous snake from India
Without a hood. *Ubiquitary*, existing everywhere.
Levirate, the code of Moses: the dead man's brother
Must marry the widow if there are no sons.
Languette, insect tongue. *Slocking stone*,
Rich ore luring investors into a worthless mine.

So, tonight The Bulls will be stronger.
In the back seat of the car Ronnie will borrow
After the game, Susan Ellen Haubner will say
Basketball players have no future.
She will dump Ronnie
For Coach Jackson's son who has, as she says,
The fine, steady hands of a surgeon.

I don't know what I want. But when the crowd
Jumps to its feet, last 30 seconds
And they roar like the engines, and they are all the tractors in Ohio
I could say one small word, Ronnie, I can say one.

A Piece of Her Dress

JEANNE E. CLARK

Aunt Ella-Elizabeth in yellow light,
Whore's hair yellow light,
Rocks in a fat and shiny chair.
She's wrapped in backstitch—
A quilt, the names of her girlfriends
And the same date on each square.
Stupid girls. Goddam. 1856.

Aunt Ella-Elizabeth on a farm of chickens
With me, her sister's kid.
Some mornings I scrape an apple,
Push it white and sweet right into her mouth.
The apple, it just sits there.

Aunt Ella-Elizabeth, I say, move your goddam mouth.
Show me some teeth.
She pulls her gray lips back then
Like a laughing dog.

Ellen, your daddy called you, Ellen,
Rubbing his forehead. Hard and yellow.
Ellen, he called you
To marry your first cousin, Harmon Grant.

There in Medina, Ohio,
Each girl gave a piece of her dress.
You all sat on wicker chairs on the porch.
Like ladies from some Presbyterian church,
You sewed a quilt-top. Full-Blown Tulips.

Ellen, cows without bells grazed
In your daddy's orchard by the main-house.
Those girls passed right by the stinking cows
Walking home. They saw your daddy in the yard. They waved.
But Harmon Grant and those goddam girls
Stopped coming. Your sister, muttering like a chicken,
She finished the quilt.

Aunt Ella-Elizabeth, now in that chair,
Lips buttoned tight as a lady's boot,
I know it's the apples,
How you like the thick taste of them a long time against your teeth.

Flying

SHULI LAMDEN

I. We're closer
to the sun.

Houses
glisten
like jewels

set
into the landscape:
diamonds,

swimming-pool
sapphires, the coral
of Spanish tile

roofs in LA.
The flight magazine
features Gilbert Abonneau,

a French photographer
come to California
for the spirit

of its light.
Like Rome, he says,
warm, and precise.

II. I know
the woman
next to me

but we don't
say hello.
We'll meet

at our destination,
nod
a half-greeting.

I am shy
to go
into the inner lives

of people,
says Abonneau.
He photographs

objects
of the kitchen:
saucers

and fruit,
a basket
of lemons

half-peeled,
the skin
dangling,

halved watermelons
and pomegranates
filled with seeds,

three long pears
like small erections
mirrored

in a polished
wooden
floor.

III. I face the sun
and follow
the glint

along the ground:
the plane's steel,
reflected.

We turn
to descend.
I see

the shadow
of the plane,
precise,

flying
through fields
below us.

We land,
touch darkness.

So Much

J. MILLS

"There's nothing as beautiful as a breast
pressed against cloth" I say and get
no reply from where you've crawled
beneath the heap of dirty laundry.

"Or the smell of a warm summer
night and cigarettes." A hand appears,
snaking through pink underwear
and almost spilling the chipped mug
of tequila, to grab the Marlboros
off the dusty floor. Smoke rings
begin to blossom from the sleeves
of the tangled denim shirts.

"The taste of a beer on a weekday
afternoon, the sight of a gas gauge
reading full, the successful swiping
of the neighbor's Sunday paper,"
I pause to spit the last
mouthful of liquor across the clothes,
remembering my mother's ritual
of soaking before washing.

"Of course, these are moments
of plenty and not—" You emerge
from the pile, having changed
during my words from jeans
to purple shorts. My running bra
crowns your head. "Like this?"
you ask and pull me down
onto our mound of stains.

Visions

J. MILLS

I.

Sometimes she feels
herself waiting
for the click, the locking
of the spheres, the snip
across her optic muscle
that will turn her eyes
three degrees and focus in
the happiness that's always
danced at her edges.

She opens herself
twice a day, checking her metal
slot where the whistling black man
with a missing finger will push in
the letter, the announcement
that will give her all
the vague things she wants.

She holds herself
rigid, sometimes
thinking a thousand
daily bits of information
have piled until one more
word will fuse and explode
everything she knows
into a searing piece of light.

Her waiting makes her
walk with careful steps
making people admire
the perfect poise
her waiting makes her.

II.

He knows someday he'll drop,
like a handful of hamburger
splattering across patio bricks,
like his father did when his heart
blew through his ribs,
like his grandfather did
from the twelfth floor ledge,
like he fantasizes.

He practices sometimes,
going limp. Driving,
pretending it's happened,
his flaccid wrists twist the car
into the waist high wheat
of a farmer's field until a rut
knocks his foot off the gas
and he must bring himself back
to life and take control.

In the lunchtime crowd, he tries
to will himself black, to crash
his body to the pavement
so when the paramedics
release his hand above his face
it will plummet effortlessly down.

He hopes there won't be any
pain in this silent and cool
absence
of pain he hopes.

Bette Davis: In Out of the Rain

MIRIAM SAGAN

Bette Davis movies, in out of the rain
All those rainy Wednesday matinees
Double features at the Castro Street Theater
I'd fold up my green paper umbrella
Come in under the gilt, art deco arc
Out of my life, my tears in cups of tea
Lovers on the peninsula, or on the beach
Sticky sand and tar on my feet
My heart was broken
Everything broke my heart—
Fuchsia garden in Golden Gate Park
Even the Chinese pharmacy with its antlers and potions.

Meanwhile, Bette Davis on the screen
In a hat, veiled, black and white
In the wrong dress everyone says is red
Ending up with diphtheria, a brain tumor
Some warning that to be a woman
Who gets her own way once or twice
Is to then start suffering for life
Still, these movies cheered me up
The sherry, staircase, shipboard, Bette Davis
This was a long time ago
Before death hit that neighborhood
Before I turned to go
Straight on into a wilder life than
Solitude, those rainy Wednesday afternoons.

Changing Your Mind in Taos

MIRIAM SAGAN

Your mind in Taos changes naturally
Baby on the bed between us
Mother, father, in the temporary
Room with the bright serape
Baby is changing and putting a foot in her mouth
When an hour ago she had not found that foot
Baby wants to suck, milk
White as the cloud on Taos mountain
Dribbling out of a corner of her mouth
I'll take you on a narrow street
Around the curve of fields
Only telephone wires tell the time
Everything else follows the sun
Strands of sunflowers, noisy flock of birds, so black
I'll show you a cow because cows have pretty eyes
Street of the martyrs under Taos mountain
But I am not Joan of Arc
If I hear voices I say: so sorry,
Can't go, I've got this baby
Who is better than any party
Peace, that's what the child's mouth says
Among the goo goo and the ga ga
Mesa is god changing god's mind
Saying plain under mountain, saying gorge, saying river
River is the thing that changes mind to stay river
I sit in the huge old bathtub in 3 inches of cool water
Baby girl, I tell you this is swimming
Swimming in a white enamel bath under Taos mountain
Women belong in bathtubs
If you are ever puzzled about being a woman
Just get into the bathtub
You will be Taos mountain
Only smaller only warmer only faster only wilder
And you can change your mind anytime you want.

How to Accommodate Men

MARILYN KRYSL

"You picked up the wine?" A asks me at breakfast. He leans on his elbows, observing my cleavage as I bend to check the muffins in the oven. I am wearing my see-through Renaissance robe with Juliette sleeves, the one A ordered for me from Night and Day Intimates.

"Wine?" I say, testing the muffins with a toothpick.

"For the party."

"Party?"

"The party for Subovsky." He sips his coffee slowly. Mornings he's slow. "A few people are coming over after Subovsky's talk. Not many, I'm keeping it small. I thought I told you. Did you forget?"

I never forget. I write things down. Even when I don't write things down, I don't forget. I remember everything A tells me. I didn't forget, but I don't say this. It would be counter-productive, and I'm geared for production.

"Maybe I did," I say. "I probably did."

"Not more than twenty," A says. "Wine and a few snacks. And get a bottle of Scotch too. Subovsky likes Scotch."

A few snacks, I think, bringing on the muffins. I can dash to the store during my lunch hour, if I time it right. Eat crackers and nuts and yogurt in the store while I shop. And while I prepare dinner I'll make a paté. A likes an elegant surprise.

"Napkins," I say. "I'll get some paper napkins." A chews a bite of muffin thoughtfully while I rush to get a pad and pencil. Someone had better make a list and it had better be me. Twenty means forty plus. They bring their wives and girlfriends, they invite an acquaintance at the last minute. Subovsky will have a local girl or two in tow. I'll get three Scotch and some gin and tonic too. Club soda, I think. Club soda, and limes.

"Club soda and limes," A says. He gets up and goes to shower and dress.

I write down limes. Toothpicks. Small paper plates. Olives and salted nuts, a tray of cold cuts and cheese. Forty means mud on the carpet, and winestains, but the carpet needs cleaning anyway. I make a note to call the cleaning service and set up an appointment. I'll vacuum, I think, while the paté bakes. Clean the bathroom. Bring out the ashtrays. And pick up aspirin for the ones who think ahead to their hangovers.

I rush around in my head as I dress, thinking of everything. Thinking of everything is my specialty. Stamina is my specialty. I get by on very little sleep, and I can eat anything. Or I can eat next to nothing, if that's what there is. I have the constitution of an ox, though I don't look like an ox. I admire my handsome face in the mirror, my head full of hair, my Simone Signoret mouth. I'm a looker, with plenty of body. A likes body, as long as it's in the right places.

The right places are another of my specialties.

"I'm going," A calls. I hurry out of the bathroom to see him off. He likes to be seen off, and I don't disappoint him. On the stand I notice his library books, overdue. He's forgetting them again. I make a note to drop them off and pay the fine on my way to work.

"Keys?" I say.

Suddenly he's worried. He pats his pocket. Then he smiles. "I've got them," he says proudly, and kisses me. I flick my tongue in his mouth, quick quick, a little reminder of things to come. A likes to be reminded. His eyes register my reminder, and then he prepares himself. To get ready for *out there*, where it's hell, he goes chilly. He focuses on something distant and above me.

"Bye," I say, holding the door open for him.

On the third step he pauses and turns back.

"Ice," he says.

My smile is tropical.

"Ice," I reply.

When a man comes on to me, I help him. "Poor baby," my mother said when her man couldn't find his socks which were in his drawer or his nail clippers which were in his pocket. "They need our help," my mother said. This was the message I drank down with my mother's milk. A man has only to look at me suggestively and I'm thinking on where can I take him, where can I lay him down. One raised eyebrow and I'm off, I'm at his service.

I am never aggressive in traffic. On planes I give men the window seat. I give them my Wall Street Journal. I give them my piece of cake. In supermarkets I let men get in line ahead of me. And I carry in the groceries myself and put them away before A gets home. I feel out what a man wants and then I give it to him. And I always, always keep my conversation clean. I don't muddy the waters with unpleasant hints that he needs self-improvement or reminders to take out the trash. I take the trash out for him.

I never ask A where he's been. I don't challenge his extenuating circumstances. I treat his extenuating circumstances as his inalienable right. It's my specialty to make allowances for extenuating circumstances. And I fill his chinks with little appreciations of his male prowess and his talent for leadership. "What a stud," I whisper in his ear. "You ought to be senator."

At the office I get the work out. I don't miss work. I don't get sick. Getting sick as a general rule throws a wrench in things. It inhibits thinking of everything. It inhibits stamina. And it gives the impression of being unreliable. Mr. Washburn knows he can rely on me, and he rewards me with regular raises, bonuses at Christmas and on my birthday, and with his expensive admiration. I say expensive because he is stingy with admiration. No one else at the office gets any. There can only be one favorite at the office, and I'm it.

Mr. Washburn thinks he admires me because I'm efficient. *She gets the work out* is how he refers to the effect I have on him. He doesn't understand that it isn't what I do but who I am that has the effect of making his work, and his life, seem easier. Simply being in my presence now makes everything seem easier to Mr. Washburn. General progress through the working day seems easier. Thinking of what to say in dictation seems easier when I take dictation. Getting up and getting showered and shaved and dressed in the mornings seems easier to Mr. Washburn, knowing I'll be there.

I make things seem easier to him than they actually are.

I have been with Mr. Washburn long enough that I no longer have to do the things I did at first. And I should add that I add an extra touch which Mr. Washburn is unaware of: I do not tempt him. Though I'm a handsome woman, I dress for work with a studied dowdiness. My clothes appear to be expensive but mute. My makeup is carefully keyed to erotic effacement. I wear my hair in a dowager's knot and I appear to be without a waist. I look like a drudge, which enhances the impression that I get the work out.

And I never sit where Mr. Washburn can see my legs.

I take it to my credit that Mr. Washburn has no idea how old I am. It has never occurred to him even to wonder.

Twenty is forty. I'm prepared. I can handle forty. I can handle sixty if need be, I've tripled the recipe. I circulate among the guests, emptying ashtrays, feeling sumptuous with preparedness. I can rein myself in or give myself full play. Be loosely flexible or graciously austere. Gay or elusive or intimately chatty. I'm prepared for the demands of the situation, and when the situation changes I'm prepared for change.

A keeps Subovsky's glass filled, and I attend to the other thirty-nine. I fill their glasses, and they confide in me. X confides he's having problems at work. He explains these problems in considerable detail. I nod sagaciously. My brow furrows ever so slightly, just enough to imply a womanly concern. I beg him to clarify the parts of his story which are still vague. I assure him I want the whole picture. Since I know the other men he refers to, I can agree, knowingly.

"Yes," I say. "You're right about Martin. Yes, he can be trying. Though you're right, he's unaware of this. And the fact that he's trying and unconscious of this fact makes it all the worse, of course. Your judgment is absolutely accurate." X begins to look happier. He becomes more animated. He considers me an outside party. He feels I am an intelligent but disinterested observer. He can trust my reaction to be objective. And now I have vindicated his views. He feels confirmed. He thinks me a remarkable woman, and his respect for his colleague A clips up several notches.

I fill his glass and move to Y. Y is disconsolate and downcast. I attempt to cheer him up, but he won't be cheered. I inquire discreetly into the cause of his gloom. He confides he's having problems at home. His wife has turned sullen, and his children are becoming unmanageable. I sympathize with the scourge of sullen wives and difficult children. I suggest possible causes, I have a bagful of possible causes handy. And I offer possible courses of action. I have quite a number of those on hand too.

Y deliberates. No, none of my suggestions will quite do the trick. I offer yet another, brightly. Y deliberates again. I attend his deliberation. I'm prepared to offer him my attentive presence for as long as it takes. He considers at length the advantages and the drawbacks of my last suggestion. At last he decides. He ought to have thought of it himself, he says. In fact he *had* thought of it, but hadn't quite countenanced his own ingenuity. Now he believes this suggestion of mine is a stroke of genius. He thanks me for reminding him of what he knew all along was the solution. He beams. He is filled with admiration for his own resourcefulness.

Now Z approaches me. His problem is epistemological. I throw practicality to the winds. We are in the rarified upper atmosphere and there is no telling when we will get back down. But I don't worry. I let him fly the plane, I'm along the for ride. He whisks me high above the abstract scenery. Herds of *ifs* and *thens*, coveys of *howevers*. Flocks of *it would seems*. Now we hover above the watering hole where at sunset these species converge.

Suddenly Z spots an opening in the tight circle around Subovsky. In the midst of a *nevertheless* he takes off. He flies away, but I do not fall to earth. I'm prepared for anything, especially for abrupt changes in elevation. I can glide along indefinitely, I can fly upside-down, I can land on a dime. Humming, I wipe up a spill. A stays at Subovsky's side.

I do a last-minute check on the well-being of those who have not been able to command Subovksy's ear.

A asks me to drive Subovksy to his hotel. Subovksy is smart as a whip and smooth as glass. He recognizes, when he meets me, that he's met his match. He asks me to come up for a nightcap. When I get back, the party is emptying out. The last guest leaves at 1:00 a.m., but A is still full of vim and vigor. Though it's late, he's been overstimulated. He's high on Subovksy's attention. He does not ask what took me so long. Instead he paces, unseeing, amidst half empty glasses set down on the carpet, the overflowing ashtrays, the scattered paper plates. He needs a climactic end to the evening. Without it he will not be able to come down.

I'm prepared. I've got a reserve tank saved especially for A, and I know what he needs. I go to him wearing an expression of passionate intensity. I let him look into my eyes. I let him kiss me on the mouth. I let him think what he's thinking.

He's thinking Subovksy. He's thinking how Subovksy took a certain, clearly discernible interest in him. How Subovksy seemed genuinely curious about A's work. How Subovksy recognized the perspicacity of A's casual remarks and laughed twice. How Subovksy followed A's line of argument thoughtfully and pointed out only two weak suppositions. How it's a sure thing that Subovksy will publish a chapter of A's new work-in-progress in his highly respected journal. And will pay tribute to A's shrewdness by recommending him for one of those grants you can't apply for. And will invite A to chair a panel next year at the international meeting in Prague.

I take A by the hand and lead him into the bedroom. I don't say a word. It might be counterproductive to interrupt his train of thought. He has just remembered that, among his many talents, is the fact that he's a hot hit with women. He remembers when he first swept me, so to speak, off my feet. How I was unable to withstand the smoldering of his sexual aura. One thing leads to another, and he remembers what a skillful lover he is generally, how capable he is of heavy duty and prolonged performance. How his wide experience has inevitably made him adept at pleasing women. And how surprised they are when he knows instinctively what they like.

I lay him down on his back and kneel between his thighs. My technique is sure fire. I am swift and deft. I keep an eye on A's face and monitor his progress, its advances and retreats, its falterings and its holding steady. I tease him out, I get him to the first level and keep him there, then I bring him along a little further. When I've got him to the edge of the first level, I go ahead, I get him up to the next. I bring him along, hand over hand, up we go. I know when to string it out, and when to speed toward the finale. I am sure of each hold, I know the way by heart. I know A by heart, his strong suits, his weak points. I have him plotted, and I have all the time in the world. I am indefatigable, if need be.

With me he's guaranteed the summit.

With me he can't fail.

I don't invite my mother to visit. I visit her, or I arrange to meet her somewhere else.

When A's mother comes, A is nervous and irritable. He has never been able to strike the right note with her. Though he says in his heart he loves her deeply, he has not succeeded in establishing satisfactory rapport. His mother's visits keep him a constant shambles. He can't enjoy his coffee at breakfast, and he can't concentrate on his work. At night he can't sleep.

She arrives with a walker, a bedpan and her own special chair. Her go systems are liberally supplemented with hose and tube. I say I'll take over. I assure A I enjoy her company. She is sharp as a tack, she doesn't miss a thing. She scolds me if the toilet needs cleaning, and she reads A's notes for his work-in-progress and pries into his calendar.

"Who's this Michele?" she demands. "Who's Rosalie?"

A puts his head in his hands. "No one you know, Mother," he says weakly.

"Michele is the dentist," I tell her. "Rosalie is his typist."

A and I lie in bed at night and whisper. Though she is deaf, she hears our voices. "I know you're talking about me," she calls out from the guest room. And she has an ear cocked for rhythmic moans of the mattress. A lies beside me, flat on his back, rigid. He grinds his teeth. He groans.

"Do something," he begs me. "Think of something."

I get up and give her her pills. I get her to swallow them with a shot of Wild Turkey. I talk up whiskey as a time tested, homeopathic remedy. "This is not one of those new fangled horrors drugs," I tell her. "Whiskey is reliable. It's been known for its healthy properties since ancient times. Mothers give it to their babies when they're teething. Pioneer women used it, and it got them all the way West."

A's mother is impressed by what she perceives as my respect for the old, my distrust of the new. She beams up at me from her bed jacket. I fill the glass again. "Drink this," I say.

Soon she's asleep. Then I take the whiskey and the glass back to our bedroom. A is sitting up in bed, a wreck.

"I've put her to sleep," I say.

"What if she wakes up again?" he says. "She always does. She never sleeps more than ten minutes at a stretch. I won't get any sleep at all tonight."

I lean over him, holding the shot glass.

"Drink this," I say, handing him the glass. He drinks it down. "She was asleep when I left," I say, filling the glass again. "She won't wake up. Drink a little more of this," I say.

"I won't be able to sleep and tomorrow will be hell," A says, downing the Wild Turkey. "How will I get through the day?"

"Trust me," I say, pouring one more. "You're going to sleep all night. You're going to sleep like a baby. You're going to wake up rested tomorrow. Tomorrow you'll feel great. Just drink a little more of this," I say.

But A is asleep.

Men like having money.

I never lend A money. I never remind A I have money. A assumes my salary is spent on clothes, the hairdresser, magazines. He assumes I make less money than I do, pocket money. We don't discuss money, and A does not think of money when he thinks of me. He has never seen me writing a check or paying the paper boy. He imagines my purse holds kleenex, lipstick, a mirror. I hide my checkbook and my credit cards in a secret pocket, just in case he looks in my purse for a book of matches.

Though I buy the groceries and pay the rent, it does not seem so. The groceries seem simply to appear, and if we run out of butter—but we don't. We'll never run out of butter.

A believes he supports me. A goes to the liquor store and buys a case each of Scotch, Bourbon, Gin. He feels like a big spender. When he pays the cashier he feels responsible. When he buys a tie or a suit, when he fills the tank of his Subaru, he imagines he's seeing to my welfare. A thinks he's thinking of me. He feels protective and generous, signing the receipt.

What I do is pay a part of A's bills on the sly. I pick bills he won't miss, charges he would rather forget. The ophthalmologist, the shrink, his account at the Wine Cellar, at *Logos*, at Subaru Sales and Service. I am careful never to pay off an account, that he would notice. Instead I slip in a payment here and there, middlesized payments, not enough to arouse suspicion, but enough to make his monthly statement a pleasant surprise. He imagines it is his own occasional payments that do this, or that he has actually spent less than it seemed. I make partial payments to Mastercharge and American Express as well, and at the end of the month A discovers he has extra cash. Extra cash makes him feel expansive. He buys me three dozen roses. He buys me a naughty black lace teddy. He buys me a cockatoo. And he takes me out to dinner five nights in a row. I lose two pounds and A gains ten. The waiters are impressed by the tips he leaves. Now he is out of cash, but he still has that rich feeling, so he makes a down payment on a tape deck for the Subaru and opens an account at Inner City Tapes and Records. He orders prescription sunglasses. And he puts a case of champagne on his account and charges a dozen new hardbacks.

The next day he comes walking in like Menelaus back with the booty. He's bought me an emerald bracelet he noticed I'd admired. I am astonished, overwhelmed.

"Oh!" I say. "You didn't! You shouldn't have!"

There is the faintest glimmer of the beginning of tears in my eyes. I put on the bracelet. I seem still overwhelmed, but A waves away my gratitude.

"There may be other little presents you'd like," he said. He suggests I make suggestions. I mention a suit I put on lay-away at Bergdorf-Goodman's. A coat. Boots. I mention a car phone, some luggage. A bikini I tried on—he was with me, he remembers the bikini. A makes a note of the other things I've mentioned. He's into providence now, and profligacy. And he becomes suddenly protective. I should be cautious, he tells me, especially at night. He looks me in the eye to make sure I get his message. Park only in well lighted areas, he tells me. Then he revises this. If I need to go out at night, from now on he'll drive me, he'll pick me up at the curb. He feels generous, he feels flush, he feels extravagantly possessive. He strides back and forth, commanding space, dominating time.

In bed A is spunky and gymnastic. He wants to try every imaginable

position. He insists on plying me with techniques. He becomes a veritable *Book of Knowledge*, and he wants his aerobic fitness confirmed.
"Like it?" he asks.
"Ummm," I say, purring.
"How about this?"
"Fantastic!" I say.
When he whips out surprises, I'm surprised. When he hopes to overwhelm me, I'm overwhelmed. The big spender is more work than the aspiring scholar, but I've got stamina, I'm prepared. And when A falls asleep, I balance my checkbook. I'm in the black.
Everything is going according to plan.

A is leaving me.
You might think I would be frantic. I'm not. When he announces he's moving out, I pretend to be surprised. He wants to surprise me. He thinks I haven't noticed his restlessness, and the scent of perfume—not mine—on his skin. And he thinks Rosalie's new fervor, increased attentiveness, and her offer to let him stay at her apartment are the result of his own irresistable attractiveness.
"Oh!" I say, my face in lovely—but not too lovely—confusion. A does not like to feel conflicted. And A does not like scenes. They irritate his peptic ulcer. They interfere with his work. They play havoc with his sleep patterns and generally disrupt his *Weltanschauung*. He gets a headache. He gets pain in his shoulders. He gets distracted and forgets to record his checks, put money in meters. And he leaves the Subaru's lights on all night.
I am careful to avoid scenes. "You're unhappy," I say, my lower lip beginning to tremble. A looks down at the floor. When he looks up, I begin to weep, quietly. Then I withdraw discreetly to the bedroom, as though I need to think this over. I close the door behind me with exaggerated care, as though, with his announcement, all things in the material world have become inexplicably fragile.
A is relieved. He wants his departure to have an effect, but not so much that he need feel guilty. I give it to him just the way he wants it. I am careful not to upset him, and anyway, I'm not upset. I'm not angry, I'm not desperate, and I'm not surprised.
I lie down and pick up the book on my side of the bed and begin chapter twenty-two. Tonight I don't have to prepare dinner. I don't have to vacuum while the paté bakes. I don't have to fill glasses and empty ashtrays, draw out A's tedious colleagues, fly upside down and land on a dime. If I'm out of butter, it's no disaster—but I'm not out

of butter. There's plenty of butter, and I am not the one who has to pack the bags, box the books, sort the medicine cabinet and the dirty laundry, find the wristwatch, the wallet, the checkbook and the missing umbrella.

Day after tomorrow I fly to Tahiti. Mr. Washburn's travel designer has arranged my three-week vacation with pay. I'll spend the first week there being wined and dined by Subovksy, enjoying my black lace teddy, my bikini. Then Subovksy will have to get back to work, and I'll spend the next two weeks bathing in the turquoise waters, admiring the emerald bracelet's shimmering in tropical twilight. When I return, tanned and rested, I may lie fallow for a while, avoid romantic attachments. I will live with the cockatoo for a while. Eventually though I'll probably look for a replacement for A. It won't be difficult to find one to my liking. There are As out there like you wouldn't believe. Forty-nine percent of the population is male, and they all need someone to triple the recipe. They need someone to make allowances for extenuating circumstances. They need someone to think of everything, and they need someone to make 62 cents every time they make a dollar, someone to help pay their bills. In a word, *accommodation*. They've become dependent on accommodation, as much of it as they can get.

What do I get out of this?

Everything.

I know everything that's going to happen before it happens. I know because I make it happen. I'm the one with the mint, with the moolah. Nothing catches me off balance, there are no surprises. I've thought of everything. Thinking of everything, remember, is one of my specialties. It's my hand on the tiller, me at the wheel. They don't move an inch I haven't foreseen and set in motion. They don't blink unless I set them blinking. They don't zip, they don't unzip. I'm the one with the leverage, the sway, the mastery, the keys, the infallible plan.

When I finish chapter twenty-two I begin chapter twenty-three. I'm in no hurry, I feel no anxiety, I'm under nobody's gun. It's A who will be distraught the next time his mother comes to visit. And when he discovers that Rosalie doesn't cook and has never emptied an ashtray. When Rosalie runs out of butter. And when he realizes how much it costs to keep Rosalie and how tricky it is to meet Michele three times a week without Rosalie finding out. And when the bills come in from Mastercharge and American Express, when he suddenly discovers he's overdrawn.

And when Subovksy does not publish an excerpt from A's work-in-progress in his highly respected journal.

When the grants are announced, and it turns out Subovksy didn't after all recommend him.

When Subovksy does not invite A to chair a panel at the international meeting in Prague.

When Subovksy meets A between sessions in the corridor and passes him as though they've never met.

Reviews

GENE FRUMKIN

Surface Tension, by Elaine Equi. Minneapolis: Coffee House Press, 1989. 69 pp., $8.95

Elaine Equi's slender poems stretch toward meaning the way a möbius strip does: they are double-edged usually, while maintaining a unified and singular flow. This might be the surface tension she had in mind when titling the book, but whatever the case, many of the poems reflect a taut energy and a raying outward. They appear to be poems of narrow range, yet they stay in the mind as a construct of funny wounds.

"Maria Callas" exemplifies Equi's way of blending wit, in its clever, amusing sense, with harshness, and fusing them into a lyric of sharp insight at the extremes of the diva's expressive range.

>   Canaries faint
>   when caged
>   by the
>   metallic ardor
>   of your voice
>
>   filing its way
>   through the bars
>
>   as if
>   you intended
>   to pluck
>   the unfinished song
>
>   from their lungs
>   and devour it.
>
>   There is still
>   a touch of
>   the ancient myths

about you
though classically trained
as wild-eyed and tragic

to the opulence
of opera
you bring

a harsh
elemental reality

vinegar stored
in an oak casket

salt poured
on an enemy's wounds.

    The movement from the fainting canaries, caged by Callas's voice—which also files its way through the bars it has erected—to the mythic background and operatic opulence shows a skill that catches a truth at the height of an artist's art. The bars of canary music, the devouring of the birds' "unfinished song," though violently put, give us the lightness, the trill, of high notes that perhaps the canaries could not have managed by themselves. This contrasts with the lower scale of "elemental reality," and the two examples thereof at the conclusion. The triteness of the last two lines is canceled out by reference to the ancient myths as circumventing the singer's classical training so that these lines have a savage edge, which follows from the idea of vengeance conveyed by the stored vinegar.

    Equi has a splendid ear, shown not only by her ability to trace out the essentials of a voice such as Callas's, but also in the sound of her poems. Note the subtle, pervasive near-assonance in "Tao."

To go
round the world
with a flair
on a matchhead

from wharf
to ant farm

observing
all the signs
by rote

sad trot
charred nettles

the dog-eared webs
that hone the ether

until and then

furtive as a werewolf
you reappear
o path

Note "world," "flair," "wharf," "farm," then later "rote" and "trot" followed by "charred" and "-eared" and "ether," the "were" of "werewolf," and finally "reappear." And then there's the path, which must be circular and have something to do with the letter "r," so ubiquitous in the poem. Of course, that is so: the "world" and "r" are both round, at least to the ear, aren't they?

Maybe the path will also lead the reader to find Equi's book, which would certainly be a sound, circular step on the way to the tao.

Unexpected Grace, by Glenna Luschei. Isla Vista, California: Turkey Press, 1989. 53 pp., $7.50

Diving Through Light, by Glenna Luschei. Pismo Beach, California: Tiger Stream Press, 1989. pp. unnumbered, limited edition of 40 copies

These poems by Glenna Luschei provide an excellent overview of work accomplished during the last two decades. While the early poems in *Unexpected Grace* catch significant glimpses of nature and human relationships, it is in the later poems of this volume and in the chapbook, *Diving Through Light*, that Luschei's voice achieves its strongest authority.

This voice is sensuous, delicate, yet it strikes quickly. It aims for essences, like the best of Oriental brushstrokes, and often enough it is on target. "Target" might seem an inappropriate word, too harsh in conjunction with the gentle intonation indicated, but the poems do have their force.

I remember your thin
white hands
how you longed to stain them crimson
blackberry picking
under the bridge

> your long fingers
> filling in your application.
> No address, no next of kin.
> You needed work.
> We took you on.
>
> You thought summer would never come.
> You left in a lightning storm
> and never came back.
>
> During winter rains
> when we cut back blackberry canes
> I think of your lifeline
> springing close to the bone
> and wonder where you went.
>
> Thorny fingers of the new plants
> grab my hand.
>
> ("Canes," *UG*, p. 46)

    The connection between nature and people, as they interweave, is made overtly here as it is in most of the other poems in both books. The compassion of one person for another is clearly defined in terms of the canes, at first through the joy in picking blackberries. Later, after the human linkage has been severed, the plants turn prickly, they act: the thorns remind by implicit tiny bloodlettings of the berries' crimson stains. The lightning storm prefigures the thorns. This is a tightly made poem, tough in its assessment of life's arrivals and departures.

    If some of Luschei's work is touched by sadness—as it is—some also moves toward serenity.

> Without ever trying
> I find myself a judge.
>
> *Spring sounds like a deer eating*
> wins the first grade poetry contest.
> *Snow falls heavy as a dictionary*
> comes in second.
>
> I track one of those bucks
> fat from a winter of daily rain
> and green manzanita
> but no snow at all.

> Let the dictionaries fall.
> I listen for the deer eating.
>
> ("Deer," *UG*, p. 47)

Much of the concern in *Diving Through Light* is with traveling; the effort to arrive at different places is also to arrive at some core, something to be brought back and situated in ongoing life. When Luschei writes in "Deck"

> There is a smell of rot
> but I no longer consider
> mind over matter.
>
> I dive through traveling light.

she gives us much more than a tourist's souvenir of the Bahamas. Here we find a structuring, a modest theory of relativity, proposed as a taking stock of self and others, of place in the psyche's environs. In the word "dive" there is a challenge, the force of being's motion within the context of a vaster, consummate movement, that of light itself. To dive, in this sense, is to dare. And to accept one's action as only a part of the world's substance and energy.

Although large matters, such as political, cultural and language questions, are not much in evidence, Luschei has shaped from her intimate archive two books her readers can enter with the assurance that they will receive generous hospitality and, even more, a pleasurable communication with a vivid poet.

Here, by Glenna Luschei. Tabula Rasa Press, 1989. pp. unnumbered, no price listed

This latest book of poems by Glenna Luschei, published in 1989, continues an ever-intensifying meditation on the forces of nature as they provide a cyclical rhythm for human life as well as a source from which to look for sustenance and enhancement. Though this book is small—25 pages including fine lino cuts by Anita Segalman—its effect is jarring in the best sense.

The first, "I Want to Be Your Poet," states succinctly in its last line a sensuous desire that situates the position of these poems. "I want to be your poet, to be your lover" is at the heart of Luschei's aesthetic.

The line is not a mere gloss, an easy, romantic clincher; it needs to be read seriously in context and also in its lighter aspect:

> I want to be your poet
> who invites you up the sweet
> smelling stairs
> as my redwood home
> would welcome the traveler,
> sun on pine needles,
> light through clerestories.
>
> I want to be the poet
> who sits through the night with you
> with the cricket calling
> cough of the kit fox
> with the rasp of the newborn word.
>
> When it's time to leave the house
> I want to be the poet
> who will weep with you.
> How beautiful
> when mock orange winds around your head.
> Redwood fences reflect the maroon
> of the crab apple
> the burgundy of flowering plum.
> Windows admit the first lip
> of morning on the blue pitcher,
> flap, flap of the bluejay in the birdbath.
>
> I want to be the poet
> who can kiss you awake.
>
> I'm not afraid of garlic breath.
> I'll deliver CPR.
> From your garden I'll pull out the onion
> with a head like Einstein.
> Get ready for a surprise!
>
> I want to be your poet, to be your lover.

"Surprise" is an apt word here; the poems do surprise consistently, in a true, satisfying way. The title poem reads:

> Love's in the daily doings
> the blister on the first roasting chili
> the race to gather sheets
> at the wick of lightning.

We fold the linen with lavender
and sage,

Love's the oar that draws us to the sea.

You propel me over quick
silver waves to San Luis Obispo,
through the spidery hills of black oak,
call me home.

The mica I bring you
scatters in my pocket,
but the Hunter Moon
tracks it to the tarmac.

Why scan the moon's two continents for love?

Our friends shout, "Look around!"

It's here beside us
on the dark side.

We fold the linen with lavender
and sage.

For me the lines "It's here beside us / on the dark side" meets the criterion of integral surprise; it has the integrity of disclosure so that the lead-up lines are suddenly confirmed and love goes beyond the "daily doings," becoming a revelation of the night, of the suppressed.

Besides writing about love and its possibilities, Luschei is also a poet of people and places. In this book, a recurring place is Albuquerque, where Luschei lived for a number of yers. And among the people is an old friend, Julie Graham, who has died in the interim and to whom the book, as well as three good poems, is dedicated. *Here* is solid, gratifying work.

A New Path to the Waterfall, by Raymond Carver, 1989. 126 pp., no price listed

This final volume of poems by Raymond Carver is not entirely a collection of *his* work; his poems are interwomen with "poetry" by Chekhov and others. Chekhov, of course, is renowned for his plays and short stories, not for any poems he might have written, so what we have in *A New Path to the Waterfall* is a rearrangement of his prose in verse lines. A connection is thereby attempted to Carver's poems—and it works beautifully. Although their themes are not especially similar, the bareness and economy, the subtlety of their compassionate vision link these writers from different times and places.

Like his Russian predecessor, Carver—who died young at 50 in August 1988—was an experiential writer. Primarily noted for his short fiction (like Chekhov, he never published a novel), Carver turned later in his career to poetry as well as fiction. He achieved success through a distinct voice that went farther than what we usually think of as realism; his work was so strong physically and mentally that it attained what I think of as tough poetry, not like Bukowski's but rather an unflinching view of human failure in the most ordinary circumstances. Some have included him under the label of "minimalism," but I don't think this is correct. His characters, including himself, are local indeed in their small, limited situations, yet they flower in a much larger garden, weeds and all.

The last section of this book is given over to poems written after the hard-smoking—and formerly hard-drinking—Carver knew he had been stricken with lung cancer. Here is "What the Doctor Said."

> He said it doesn't look good
> he said it looks bad in fact real bad
> he said I counted thirty-two of them on one lung before
> I quit counting them
> I said I'm glad I wouldn't want to know
> about any more being there than that
> he said are you a religious man do you kneel down
> in forest groves and let yourself ask for help
> when you come to a waterfall
> mist blowing against your face and arms
> do you stop and ask for understanding at those moments
> I said not yet but I intend to start today
> he said I'm real sorry he said
> I wish I had some other kind of news to give you
> I said Amen and he said something else
> I didn't catch and not knowing what else to do
> and not wanting him to have to repeat it
> and me to have to fully digest it
> I just looked at him
> for a minute and he looked back it was then
> I jumped up and shook hands with this man who'd just given me
> something no one else on earth had ever given me
> I may even have thanked him habit being so strong

This poem is typical of Carver's last work, with its grim, Bogartian humor. Throughout the book he weighs irony against the experiential facts, his own and others'. Irony is the only habit that works, that and humor. His work adds up to something major, even if one decided that the poem quoted wasn't really poetry but instead a kind of uncapitalized, unpunctuated prose. But I don't believe that's true; the rhythmical force of his lines matter too much. I don't think one could sensibly reverse the process attempted with Chekhov's prose. Although the tone, the style, the humor are similar, Carver's poems would not succeed as other than what they are. In any case, the labels don't matter in the face of the concise truths that sum up to so harrowingly close a view of what an enormous job it is to be fully human.

Good Books, Briefly

PATRICIA CLARK SMITH

Editor David Jones' own experience as director, theater historian, and literary critic make *New Mexico Plays* more than just a good regional anthology. Jones gives us a lucid introduction to the long tradition of New Mexico performance art and his anecdotal prefaces on each of these six contemporary plays set them and their authors in their personal and cultural context. (University of New Mexico Press, 1989. $18.95 paper, 231 pages.) Rudolfo Anaya, like Jones, has put together an anthology whose authors range from the very familiar (Simon Ortiz, Tony Hillerman, John Nichols) to relative newcomers. As in Jones' collection, there is little moonlight-over-adobe romanticism to be found in *Tierra: Contemporary Short Fiction of New Mexico*. But there is real romance, as well as phone booths outside Stuckey's, mining accidents, genuine wisepersons, visions of Sandia Lab post-apocalypse, a splendid Acoma coyote and a few bilingual ghosts. (Cinco Puntos Press, 1989. $12.95 paper, 272 pages.) *Caesar of Santa Fe* is Tim McCurdy's roaring historical novel of passion and power politics during the, well, let's say *rocky* seventeenth-century administration of Governor Luis de Rosas. (Amador Publishers, 1989. $9.00 paper, 93 pages.) Jim Sagel's bilingual *On the Make Again/Otra Vez en la Movida: New and Collected Poems* brings us more of Sagel's moving, sometimes hilarious inside-outsider visions of multicultural Española Valley lives; Sagel brings to his writing the gifts of a flawless ear, fine-tuned irony, and a generous heart. (West End Press, 1989. $8.95 paper, 93 pages.) Skeet McAuley's unsentimental photographs of reservation people and land in *Sign Language: Contemporary Southwest Native America* are splendid in themselves, and beautifully complemented with an introduction by N. Scott Momaday and essays by Navajo storyteller Mike Mitchell, Navajo poet Luci Tapahonso, and photographic historian Martha Sandweiss. An Anglo critic (self-appointed) once complained to Tapahonso that she ought not to have depicted Navajo children watching TV cartoons in one of her poems; McAuley's photographs of kids at carnivals and natural gas refineries amidst mesas may not be the coffee table book on "The Indians" most tourists will seek out, but I cannot name an Anglo photographer since Laura Gilpin in her time who captures so beautifully and provocatively "the way it is." (Aperture Press, 1989. $29.95 cloth, 78 pages.)

Notes on Contributors

Alicia Gaspar de Alba is a native of El Paso but since 1986 has lived in Boston, where she teaches composition to ESL students. Bilingual Press published her first book of poems, *Beggar on the Cordoba Bridge*, in 1989 and will be publishing her first collection of short stories, *The Mystery of Survival and Other Stories*.

Michael Arvey teaches creative writing courses through correspondence study at the University of Colorado, Boulder. He is a free-lance writer and is working on his fifth young adult nonfiction book for Greenhaven Press (Minneapolis).

Tricia Baatz is a graduate student studying literature and creative writing at Hamline University in St. Paul, Minnesota. She is the recipient of the 1989 Loft-Mcknight Award in Creative Prose and has had work appear in *Streamlines*. She is currently working on a novel, *Blackbird Fly*.

Susan Barnett lives in Kaneohe, Hawaii. Her poems have appeared in *Lake Superior Review, Midwest Review*, and *Rainbird*. In 1988 she won first prize for fiction in the National League of Pen Women (Hawaii Chapter) writing contest.

Sandra Blystone lives in El Paso, Texas with her husband and two sons and teaches composition at the University of Texas at El Paso. Recent publication credits include *The Beloit Poetry Journal, Calyx, The Other Side, Eleven: A Poetry Review*, and *The Rio Grande Review*.

Maisha Baton is a poet and playwright whose works have appeared in *Afterimage, Shooting Star Review, The Black Collegiate Magazine*, and *Rio Grande Writer's Chap Book*. She is currently teaching Women's Studies at the University of New Mexico.

Eryc Bourland has been writing seriously for about a day now. He is bashful and peace loving and he'll kill anyone who says differently. Long ago he realized, with diluted elation, the lucidity and wit of the melancholy.

Robert Burlingame is on a leave of absence from the University of Texas at El Paso putting together a new book of poetry. He is anthologized in several works, including *The Pushcart III*. His work has also appeared in the *Massachusetts Review, Kansas Quarterly,* and *Bloomsbury Review.*

Albino Carrillo received a BA in creative writing from the University of New Mexico and attended the University of Arizona's MFA program. He has previously published or has work forthcoming in *Puerto del Sol, Crowdancing, The Midnight Lamp, Caliban,* and *The Great River Review.*

J. Dianne Duff, a native of New Mexico, studied theology at the University of New Mexico and now manages a family business in Albuquerque. Her poetry and fiction have appeared in *The Rio Grande Writers Quarterly, Wildflower, Southwest Discoveries,* and *The Rio Grande Writers Chapbook Series.*

Martha Elizabeth is the recipient of the Dobie-Paisano Fellowship given by the Texas Institute of Letters and the University of Texas at Austin. Her work has been published in *Passages North, The MacGuffin,* and *Concho River Review.*

Joel Frederich is a former Santa Fe high school teacher who has his roots in Iowa. He has recently moved to Missoula, Montana, where he is working in a bookstore and participating in writing workshops.

Carlos Nicolas Flores is currently the writer-in-residence at the University of the Americas in Puebla, Mexico. *The Rio Grande Review, Americas Review, Passing Through: An Anthology of Southwestern Writers,* and *Cuentos Chicanos* are some of the publications in which his work appears.

Mark Funk, poet and painter, lives and works in Albuquerque. He has published a chapbook, *My Myopia: Poems and Drawings by Mark Funk* (Manifest Destiny Press).

Bayita Garoffolo has had her work published in *Conceptions Southwest* and *Other Voices.* She teaches Spanish at Albuquerque Academy.

Penelope Gillen, who is of Otoe, Kiowa, and Irish descent, lives in Santa Fe where she writes poetry, fiction, and prose.

Sylvia Giron is from Santa Fe, New Mexico. She is studying creative writing at the University of New Mexico.

Ray Gonzalez, author and editor, is Literature Director of The Guadalupe Cultural Arts Center in San Antonio, Texas. His *Twilights and Chants* won a Four Corners Book Award in 1988, the same year he received a Colorado Governor's Award for Excellence in the arts.

David E. Hailey, Jr. is pursuing his MA degree in creative writing at the University of New Mexico. "Compressions" is his second fiction publication.

Joy Harjo was born in Tulsa in 1951 and is a member of the Creek Tribe. She received her MFA in Creative Writing from the Iowa Writer's Workshop in 1978. She has published three books of poetry and has a fourth, *In Mad Love and War,* forthcoming from Wesleyan University Press in Spring, 1990. She is an Associate Professor in the Department of English at the University of Arizona in Tucson.

James Hoggard is the author of two novels and four collections of poems. A new collection of his translations is due out in 1990. He has also had seven of his plays produced. He is a former NEA fellow and teaches English at Midwestern State University in Wichita Falls, Texas.

Thomas Alan Holmes currently lives in Tuscaloosa, Alabama, where he is completing doctoral work in English. He has served as fiction editor for *The Black Warrior Review,* and his work has recently appeared in *The Florida Review* and *The Southern Historian.*

Jeane Jacobs is of Choctaw, Cherokee and Irish descent. She is a storyteller as well as a published writer, and her fiction and poetry have appeared in *Women for All Seasons, Bishinik* (a Choctaw Newspaper), and *Women and Their Animals, Volume Two.*

Jeffrey N. Johns lives in South Korea where he works as an engineer. His stories have appeared in *Festivals* magazine and *Cross Timbers Review.*

Judi Lynn Judy is pursuing a degree in creative writing with a minor in modern dance at the University of New Mexico. Besides writing, she is interested in performance art and has produced several pieces.

Marilyn Krysl teaches at the University of Colorado and has just completed a new novel, *Atomic Open House*. Her work has appeared in *The Nation*, *The Atlantic*, *O. Henry Prize Stories*, and the *Pushcart Anthology*.

Shuli Lamden's poems have appeared in the *California Quarterly* and *Poets On*. She teaches English at Santa Fe Community College.

Carmela Delia Lanza was a winner of the 1986 recipients of the University Poetry Prize by the Academy of American Poets and Columbia University. Her poems are published in *The Worcester Review*, *Conceptions Southwest*, and *Turnstile*.

Mercedes Lawry works for a child advocacy organization and has published children's stories. Her poetry has been published by *Southern Poetry Review*, *Negative Capability*, *Sycamore Review*, and *Mid-American Review*.

James Mackie is waiting for poetic inspiration in Richmond, Virginia. He is an alcohol rehabilitation counselor and working on his MSW degree at Virginia Commonwealth University.

Miriam McCluney teaches creative writing at Albuquerque Academy and also specializes in Shakespeare. She has just completed ten years as sponsor/editor of *Other Voices*, the Academy's literary magazine.

Gabriel Melendez currently teaches at Mills College in Oakland, California and has published articles on Chicano Literature and Culture and the contemporary Mexican Novel. His poetry and fiction have appeared in *Writer's Forum*, *Voces*, and *Tierra: Contemporary Short Fiction of New Mexico*.

Melissa Miller is a graduate student in English at the University of Hawaii. Besides her interest in poetry, she specializes in the literature of indigenous Pacific Islanders and is the founder and editor of *Pacific Island Voices: A Literary Newsletter*.

J. Mills, who lives in Albuquerque, is 5'10" with thinning hair. "Well, he's the poetic type," says his fiancée's father, "but don't get me wrong—he knows his sports."

Deborah Muldavin is a poet and ecologist living in Las Cruces, New Mexico whose work has previously appeared in *Puerto Del Sol* and *Whole Notes*.

Mahlon Murphy is a paramedic and carpenter in Chama, New Mexico. He is working on a novel based on his experience as an underground miner in the mid-70s.

L. V. Quintana is a native New Mexican living in California and working on a book of poetry titled *My Hair Turning Gray Among Strangers*.

Henry Rael has published fiction in *Conceptions Southwest* and in 1988 won the D. H. Lawrence Short Fiction Writing contest. He is a student of English and political science at the University of New Mexico.

David Ray, an English professor at the University of Missouri–Kansas City, has published more than a dozen books of poetry. His recent work can be read in *The New Republic, Stiletto, Plowshares, College English,* and *Kansas Quarterly.*

Roy Ricci splits his time between Albuquerque and "Da Bronx," preferring sagebrush to subways and coyotes to citified congestion.

Harvena Richter, a former creative writing teacher at the University of New Mexico, is now writing full-time. She is working on a book on her father's philosophical theories, as well as fiction and poetry.

Wilma Rodriguez is a junior at New Mexico State University majoring in English. After earning her degree she hopes to join a publishing house and continue her interest in multilingual poetry.

Levi Romero is a 28-year-old native of Dixon, New Mexico.

James Ruppert, an ex-New Mexican, now teaches at the University of Alaska-Fairbanks. He gets his chile shipped to him and the moose wander into his backyard.

Miriam Sagan has recently produced a cassette tape *Poetry Devils* (1989), a fiction chapbook, *Paths to the Nudist Beach* (Samisdat 1989), a book of poetry, *Acequia Madre: Through the Mother Ditch* (Adastra 1988), and a daughter Isabel (1/20/89).

Layle Silbert has published in the *Denver Quarterly, Minnesota Review* and *West Branch* magazines. Her book of stories, *Imaginary People & Other Strangers,* was published by Exile Press in 1985.

James Thomas Stevens, a 23-year-old writer of Mohawk and Welsh descent, is a creative writing major at the Institute of American Indian Arts in Santa Fe, New Mexico.

Brian Swann has edited a number of volumes on Native American Literature and has published poetry, short fiction, and translations. He teaches at The Cooper Union in New York City.

Laura Tohe is a wandering Navajo who made her way to the Great Plains of Nebraska where she lives and teaches at the University of Nebraska-Lincoln. She is the author of *Making Friends with Water.*

Anthony Wallace is presently seeking an MA degree in creative writing from the University of Hawaii-Manoa. His work has appeared in *Wind Magazine, The Small Pond Magazine of Literature,* and other small press publications.

John Martinez Weston, a graduate student in English at the University of New Mexico, served in the U.S. Army from 1968–1971, including a combat tour in Viet-Nam in 1969. He and his wife live in Tijeras, New Mexico and recently celebrated the birth of their second child.

Peter Wild is involved in researching the life and work of Rutgers University professor John C. Van Dyke who at the turn of the century wrote the first book to celebrate, rather than condemn, the Southwest's deserts.

Christopher Woods lives in Houston. He is the author of a novel *The Dream Patch,* and a chapbook of poems, *Houses and Fugues.* His play, *Moonbirds,* was recently premiered by Stage Two Theatre Company in Illinois.